WHY NOT YOU?

BELIEVING
WHAT GOD
BELIEVES
ABOUT YOU

ED NEWTON

WHY NOT YOU?

BELIEVING WHAT GOD BELIEVES ABOUT YOU

W PUBLISHING GROUP

Published in Nashville, Tennessee, by W Publishing, an imprint of Thomas Nelson, 501 Nelson Place, Nashville, TN 37214, USA. W Publishing and Thomas Nelson are registered trademarks of HarperCollins Christian Publishing, Inc.

Published in association with The Fedd Agency, www.thefeddagency.com

Thomas Nelson titles may be purchased in bulk for educational, business, fundraising, or sales promotional use. For information, please email SpecialMarkets@ThomasNelson.com. Any internet addresses, phone numbers, or company or product information printed in this book are offered as a resource and are not intended in any way to be or to imply an endorsement by Thomas Nelson, nor does Thomas Nelson vouch for the existence, content, or services of these sites, phone numbers, companies, or products beyond the life of this book.

Unless otherwise noted, Scripture quotations are taken from the ESV® Bible (The Holy Bible, English Standard Version®). Copyright © 2001 by Crossway, a publishing ministry of Good News Publishers. All rights reserved.

Scripture quotations marked KJV are taken from the King James Version. Public domain.

Scripture quotations marked NIV are taken from the Holy Bible, New International Version®, NIV®. Copyright © 1973, 1978, 1984, 2011 by Biblica, Inc.® Used by permission of Zondervan. All rights reserved worldwide. www.zondervan.com. The "NIV" and "New International Version" are trademarks registered in the United States Patent and Trademark Office by Biblica, Inc.®

ISBN 978-1-4003-5089-6 (audiobook)
ISBN 978-1-4003-5088-9 (eBook)
ISBN 978-1-4003-5087-2 (TP)

Library of Congress Control Number: 2025939598

Printed in the United States of America

25 26 27 28 29 LBC 5 4 3 2 1

To Chuck Yates

Though we are different in many ways, we have so much in common in the Spirit. You saw past my insecurities and spoke a challenge that changed everything: Why Not You?

Your unwavering conviction in what God believes about me became a catalyst for courage and calling. This book is a testament to that truth.

CONTENTS

FOREWORD

I CONSIDER IT A HIGH HONOR TO MINISTER IN THE SAME CITY AS Dr. Ed Newton. We share a love for San Antonio. We share a call to the local church, a high appreciation for preaching, and—get this—we even share the same tattoo artist.

Ed and his family are easy to love. Their joy is contagious and vulnerability infectious. The fine people of Community Bible Church are in good hands under the leadership of Pastor Ed.

I just did what I urge you to do. I read this book.

Goodness! I am better because of it! Each page spoke to my heart. I'm confident you will say the same. Who hasn't asked the questions Ed addresses? Who hasn't wondered *Why me?* Who hasn't questioned their ability to fill God's call? Who hasn't battled insecurities?

Reading Ed's fine book brought a memory to mind.

Turn to the sports section of the 1970 Andrews High School yearbook from Andrews, Texas, and study the picture of the freshman basketball team. Not the Varsity or Junior Varsity, but the ninth-grade team. You'll find two photographs, one of the first string and one of the second team. I was on the second team. Well, almost.

The B-team had ten uniforms and twelve players. Hence, two of us didn't get to suit out for the second-team freshman games. The other no-uniform kid had thick glasses and a rotund girth. At least he had an excuse. I had decent eyesight and height, but the coordination of a rhinoceros. So in the school picture, I appear in cuffed Levi's and Hush Puppies.

I didn't want to go to the photo shoot. Capture on film my place at the bottom of the pecking order? No thanks. But just as I didn't know how to pick and roll on the court, I didn't know how to sneak out of the gym. The photographer positioned the team beneath the basket and asked the chubby kid and me to stand on either flank.

Click.

My place as a basketball nobody was documented for the ages.

You can likely relate. We all can. Insecurities haunt everyone. Thanks to God, they don't have to dominate everyone. Ed has packed these pages with inspiration and direction. It's ours for the taking.

Let's do just that.

—MAX LUCADO,
NEW YORK TIMES BESTSELLING AUTHOR AND PASTOR

WHAT'S YOUR PERSPECTIVE?

IN THE SPRING OF 2010 I PULLED UP TO CAMP EAGLE, A RETREAT center about two hours outside of San Antonio. I was there for "Mancation," Community Bible Church's men's retreat, where I was the main speaker. And I was late.

I was a traveling evangelist at the time, but I hadn't spent much time in Texas aside from a work event at SeaWorld, and Shamu was nowhere in sight at Mancation. I looked around at my surroundings and saw men from every walk of life. Rough-and-tumble Texans, put-together businessmen, ballers, hunters, both young and old. Every color and creed seemed to be represented. It was different from any event I'd spoken at before, eclectic and unique. I think heaven will look a lot like that.

The only person I didn't see was someone who looked like me. Skinny jeans, flat bill cap with hair to my shoulders (the glory days). Oh, and let's not forget about the deep V-neck T-shirts I was so fond of at the time.

I am from Florida, but I felt like I had arrived in a foreign country where the language was trucks, tacos, and guns. I both loved it *and* felt my insecurities welling up inside. The camp was situated off a long eight-mile dirt road in the middle of nowhere with no cell service, so I couldn't have called for help if I'd wanted to.

All of this was running through my mind as I walked up to the pavilion where the service had already started. Then I met Chuck.

Chuck Yates was a missionary to the one-percenters, otherwise known as the motorcycle gangs of America. His group was called the Tribe of Judah, proudly displayed on his leather jacket. He had gauges in his ears, a white goatee, and tattoos that were a result of a seasoned life.

I don't know if it was something I said or if he could supernaturally sense the anxiety and insecurities I was battling, but Chuck approached me, kissed me on the cheek, and wrapped his leather-clad arms around me. His jacket pressed into my face, and he gave me a warm, wide smile. My eyes filled up with tears, and acceptance flooded my soul from the kindness of this man I had just met.

Chuck pulled back and looked me in the eyes with a finger pointed at my chest.

"You are meant to be here, Ed. God wants to use you, and He picked you for this. Stop asking, 'Why me?' God wants to use somebody to speak His message to these men—Why Not You?"

He smiled at me again, that big, warm smile.

Up to that point in my life, I don't think I had ever had someone so directly speak what I needed to hear in a particular moment. When Chuck asked me that question, it gave me pause, not because it was wildly profound (although to me it was) but because he was demonstrating a belief in me that I didn't have in myself.

The insecurities I'd carried as I was about to preach to that group of seven hundred men began to fade because God knew I needed a word of encouragement from a man who was so different from me, down to the shoes he wore on his feet.

While this book contains stories from my life, it isn't about me; it's about you and the unseen potential that lies within you. It's about challenging the status quo, breaking the shackles of self-doubt, and stepping into the realm of possibilities where the only question that matters is, Why Not You?

Too often, we let our fears, insecurities, and the views of others overshadow what God has placed within us and desires to draw out of us. We hesitate to step into the possibility that our lives were made for so much more. Instead, we question our God-given abilities and doubt their worth. We compound this pit of despair by wallowing in self-loathing questions of discontentment, asking, *Why me?* Or we look at someone else's life and think, *God could never use me like He does them.*

Everyone, at some point in their lives, grapples with feelings of inadequacy, insecurity, and uncertainty. But when these feelings become the framework through which we interpret all of life, self-doubt becomes a debilitating mindset that robs us of realizing our true potential and the fulfillment of what God has declared and decreed over us.

There are numerous reasons why self-doubt creeps into our lives. It could be due to past failures, harsh criticism, unrealistic societal expectations, or even our inner critic that constantly tells us we're not good enough. And often, in the midst of this internal turmoil, we forget a fundamental truth that God has woven into our existence: We are made in His image, and He believes in our worth, potential, and capabilities, even when we don't.

But what if we turned the question around? What if, instead of asking, *Why me?* we began asking, *Why not me?* What if we started believing in our God-given potential and stopped seeing ourselves through the lens of our internal insecurities or the external limitations others have placed upon us?

Overcoming self-doubt is not a quick fix; it's a continuous, multiple-times-a-day journey of self-growth and spiritual development. This new beginning will require patience, perseverance, and, above all, faith in God's belief in you, even when you struggle to believe in yourself. As we venture into the heart of this book, we will dive deep into negative, self-inflicted thoughts and paralyzing beliefs about ourselves. I seek to provide practical and biblical insights to help you conquer self-doubt and align your beliefs with God's belief in you.

My aim is to help you shift your perspective, to see yourself the way God sees you and fully live in the confidence that only comes from knowing Him. You may believe the very best about others but not yourself. You may speak blessing over so many others but not yourself. And if you are honest, you may have never spoken the negative words you've spoken over yourself to anyone, not even your worst enemy. There is seldom anyone harder on you than *you*.

This book is a call for self-doubt to stop and for God-given flourishing to

> IF GOD BELIEVES IN US, WHO ARE WE TO DOUBT OURSELVES?

begin within you. If God believes in us, who are we to doubt ourselves?

Together, we will explore the question, Why Not You? to inspire you to become a living testimony of God's goodness and faithfulness, for the greater good to be accomplished in you, through you, for you, for others, and for His glory. God is looking for someone to overflow the blessing of His presence as a testimony of His love and power. So Why Not You?

Even in this moment, you may be thinking this is not for you but for someone else. I'm here to tell you that the goodness and faithfulness of God is not just reserved for others but is a promise for you as well. What if we could break free from our constraints and embrace a different perspective? What if we dared to believe about ourselves what God believes about us?

Each chapter of this book is designed to raise the hard questions, and I challenge you to be courageous enough to answer them. We will explore the common insecurities that plague us and reveal how they often originate from our wiring and the environments that shaped us, typically bringing forth cultural pressures, past traumas, and negative narratives on repeating loops in our minds.

Through introspective journal entries from my own soul and thought-provoking questions I have asked myself, I will guide you through the honest pursuit of becoming comfortable in your own skin and push you toward a deeper understanding of your unique worth and purpose.

But this book is not just about self-reflection; it is about embracing a divine perspective. We cling to scriptural truths that reveal God's unconditional love, His belief in our abilities, and His desire for us to live a life of purpose and fulfillment. As we align our beliefs with His, He will launch us into supernatural transformation that marks us for the greater good, now and forever.

This book doesn't offer a one-size-fits-all solution. It is a journey of self-discovery and faith, filled with both challenges and victories. As you turn the pages, you will be encouraged to confront your insecurities head-on, to let go of the limitations that have held you back, and to step into the abundant life that God has prepared for you.

If you're sure about who you are and wake up every day confident in your purpose, you can stop reading now; this book isn't for you. But if you have ever questioned your worth, felt stunted by rejection, or wondered if you are capable of more, keep reading.

This is your invitation to embrace the truth God sees in you, to embark on a journey of denying self-doubt and choosing to walk in empowerment and purpose. It may be a struggle at first—we tend to resist changing the habits and thought patterns we've developed over time. But if you will commit to the work, I assure you it will be well worth it.

God is going to use someone to walk in purpose, meaning, destiny, and anointing. So, I ask you, Why Not You?

CHAPTER 1

WHY ME?

DO YOU KNOW THAT GOD IS CALLING YOU TO DO SOMETHING greater than anything you have ever imagined for yourself? That's right, God has special and unique plans for your life that far exceed anything you could dream up on your own, specifically designed for you to live out.

We all know that God can and will do amazing things. Unfortunately, if you are anything like me, you often think those amazing plans are for others. You think God wants to use those around you, but certainly not you. You think, *Why would God use me? If He wants to do something extraordinary, He probably wants to choose someone who is extraordinary. I don't have what God needs to do something special.*

But that is rarely how God operates. Instead, He likes to take the ordinary person and do extraordinary things. That is how He gets the glory. If God chooses someone who already has the ability and talent to do it, who gets the credit? He isn't looking for someone with ability but availability.

If that's you, I have good news: You don't need to be qualified. God will qualify you. You just need the willingness to let God lead you wherever He chooses. God wants *you* to carry out His special plan and purpose for your life.

Now is the point where you ask the inevitable question, "But, Ed, why me?"

Well, you are not the first person to ask this question. Moses asked the exact same question when God instructed him to lead the Israelites out of slavery in Egypt into the promised land, fulfilling His long-ago promise to Abraham. He wanted Moses to be that man; God had a significant purpose for him.

THE BACKSTORY

I want to give a little context to Moses' story found in Exodus 3. Shortly after Moses was born, his mother, Jochebed, saved his life from a genocide where all newborn boys were murdered. When he was three months old, she put him in a basket in the reeds of the Nile River, not to get rid of him but to strategically place him in the waters where Pharaoh's daughter bathed.

After Pharaoh's daughter heard the cry of a baby, she saw the basket floating with Moses inside. Her servants asked who would care for this helpless baby, and she decided she would be Moses' caretaker. It was here that Moses' life was spared.

Moses, a Hebrew by birth, grew up in Egyptian culture. He walked and talked like an Egyptian. (Yes, I just quoted an '80s song.¹) He was indoctrinated and educated like an Egyptian. His entire life, he only knew how to act and live like the Egyptian people.

Egypt's Most Wanted
Fast-forward to forty-year-old Moses, who decided to step in when he caught an Egyptian man oppressing a Hebrew man.

Moses ended up killing the Egyptian and burying him in the sand, thinking all along he was serving God in doing so.

The next day, he broke up a fight between two Hebrews by basically saying, "Can we all just get along?" (Exodus 2:13, my paraphrase). When one of the men recognized Moses, he asked Moses if he was going to kill them just like he killed the Egyptian.

Moses went from living the good life in the palace to becoming Egypt's most-wanted man. He ran to a place where no one would ever find him. And there, everything changed in Moses' life.

God Calls Moses

I want you to understand something: When Moses ran, the Egyptians could not find him. But when you run to a place where no one else can find you, God knows right where you are. That's where God met Moses.

But He didn't stop there. He divinely interrupted Moses' life, using a burning bush to get his attention and talk directly to him. I don't know if you have ever processed this. God began to speak something to Moses he never would have imagined hearing: "I have heard the cries of my people; their affliction has come to Me. I want to send you back to deliver My people from bondage to the Egyptians. Tell Pharaoh to let My people go" (Exodus 3:7–10, my paraphrase).

At that moment, you would think Moses would be like, "Yes! This is my destiny! I grew up Egyptian. I know the hierarchy. I know the policies. I know the culture. I know the language. I'm the right guy for God to use supernaturally." Instead, Moses gave God five excuses why He should choose someone else for the job.

These are excuses we all can relate to because we use them when God calls us to something great in our own lives. We pray for God to use us in amazing ways. We ask that God fulfill His purpose in our lives. We hope that what God has for us will be life-changing and life-giving. But when God is ready to use us, ready to show us His purpose, all of a sudden, we are full of excuses, just as Moses was when God called him.

WHY ME?

Make no mistake, what God wanted to do through Moses was big. For Moses, it was too big, because the first question he asked God was, "Why me?" He said in Exodus 3:11, "Who am I that I should go to Pharaoh and bring the children of Israel out of Egypt?"

You might be asking what Moses meant when he asked this. Essentially Moses was saying, "I am not enough." Moses believed he couldn't lead the Hebrews out of Egypt into the promised land.

Perhaps God has called you to do something incredible, and you are asking the same question: "God, why me? I am not enough." I've asked that many times in my life.

When I was ten years old, I remember interpreting for my deaf parents at McDonald's. I had just finished ordering a Big

Mac and a Combo Meal for them and a Happy Meal for me. I took a step back from the counter, and suddenly, a sweet woman put her hand on my shoulder. Without introducing herself, she asked, "Do you do this everywhere you go?"

I responded, "Yes, ma'am."

She asked again, "So you order for your parents everywhere you go?"

I replied, "Yeah, and I talk for them all the time. I have to interpret meetings, doctors' visits, all kinds of things. I explain to people everywhere we go that I am their voice, because they can't hear."

In that moment, the woman smiled at me, and I could tell she was about to say something significant. She looked me directly in the eyes and said, "One day God's going to greatly use you."

Remember, I was ten at the time. You might be thinking, *What a life-changing moment.* But when you are ten, you're only thinking about what toy you'll get in the Happy Meal you just ordered. I didn't realize it in that moment, but years later I understood that the experiences of my upbringing were preparing me for God's calling as a lead pastor at Community Bible Church in San Antonio.

We often fail to recognize that God has prepared us for His calling long before we know what that calling is. The day that God makes it abundantly clear, you might be amazed, you might be caught off guard, and you might have a million questions. It might even feel like it came out of left field. But not to God, who wants us to understand three things:

1. Your upbringing has prepared you.
2. Your experiences burden you for similar challenges.
3. Your mistakes have not disqualified you.

God has been laying the groundwork for the incredible ways He will one day use you. He arranged (or allowed) circumstances in your upbringing that would serve as guides and reference points for your purpose. He placed a burden on you for helping others with similar experiences in ways you could not imagine. And no matter what mistakes you made along the way, these do not and have not disqualified you from God's calling on your life.

The question is not, "Why me, God?" The real question is, "Why *not* me?" When you begin to understand how the God of the universe has already prepared you and sees you, you will know that even if you have disqualified yourself, He has chosen you. The calling and purpose He has placed on your life was specifically made for you, and He will provide everything you need to accomplish it.

YOUR UPBRINGING HAS PREPARED YOU

You might be thinking, *Ed, you don't know me. You don't understand. There is no reason God would call me or choose me to do anything of significance.* And you might be right about the first part. I don't know you. But I do know that the circumstances, events, trials, and tribulations you have faced in life have prepared you for what God wants to lead you to.

In the 2008 fiction movie *Slumdog Millionaire*, an eighteen-year-old boy appeared on a game show, similar to India's version of *Who Wants to Be a Millionaire*. To win the game, he had to answer twelve questions correctly, then he would win a large sum of cash.

The boy answered all the questions correctly, but he was accused of cheating. When questioned by the police, he gave detailed descriptions of twelve events in his life that enabled him to answer each question correctly. In other words, because he learned from random life events that seemed meaningless at the time, he was able to win a huge cash prize.[2]

This does not mean that God intends you to use your life events to win a bunch of money (though who knows what God has in store for you!). But it does mean that the circumstances you face and even the events that seem insignificant all have a purpose in your life.

When you ask, "Why me?" God responds, *I have prepared you for this exact calling because of X, Y, and Z that you have gone through. Because of how each circumstance changed your life, you are exactly the person to fulfill this calling. Why Not You?*

YOUR EXPERIENCES BURDEN YOU FOR OTHERS

Not only has God allowed or engineered circumstances in your past to prepare you for His call, but He has burdened you to use those experiences to help others facing similar struggles.

I mentioned earlier that your life events and circumstances

are not random or insignificant. That is because God uses them to shape and change you or to shape and change others. Growth does not happen in comfort. Though our human brains love to keep us comfortable, God will often allow or even design circumstances that remove us from our comfort zones and force us to grow. These circumstances can be wildly uncomfortable, but God knows that through the discomfort He is conforming us into the person He will one day use for a great calling.

At other times, it is not about us at all. God allows us to face problems so we can guide others through similar terrain. Events like this can be difficult as we are enduring them. We question God. We don't understand His purposes. But in these instances, He is looking forward to who we'll help in the future. Your experiences will burden you for others, and it is your job not to waste them but to use them to help those God places in your life along the way.

YOUR MISTAKES DO NOT DISQUALIFY YOU

Now, this might be the point when you say, "Hold up, Ed, I got you. I know God is calling me to something significant. I know that my upbringing has prepared me for it, and I have a burden because of the experiences I have gone through. But you don't understand. I have made some serious mistakes, ones I don't think God can forgive. There is no way God wants to use me to do something incredible."

Is that you? Are you saying that today? Maybe you have said that before. If so, I have good news for you: Your mistakes do not disqualify you from God's amazing call on your life.

All throughout the Bible you will find stories of broken people, sinners, who God used to do things so incredible that we still read and preach about them thousands of years later. These were all people who made mistakes. They disobeyed God, and they got off track in their faith journeys. And you know what? God forgave them. But more than that, He turned them around and used them to do the unthinkable. That is what God does. He takes ordinary people and does extraordinary things. Remember, God does not look at your ability, just your availability.

YOUR MISTAKES DO NOT DISQUALIFY YOU FROM GOD'S AMAZING CALL ON YOUR LIFE.

God does not disqualify you because of your mistakes, because it is not about you; it's about Him. Think of King David, whose lineage God used to fulfill His covenant. David slept with another man's wife, had that man killed in battle, lied about it, and took the woman to be his wife (2 Samuel 11–12). Sounds like a few (big) mistakes, right? But God didn't disqualify David. In fact, God went as far as to have Jesus descend from David's family line.

My friend, you cannot out-sin God's grace. There is nothing you can do to remove yourself from a place of God's forgiveness. When He forgives, He turns us around and uses us to do remarkable things.

"Why me?" you ask. Let's change the question to "Why *not* me?"

CHAPTER 2

WHO MADE
YOUR MOUTH?

NOW THAT WE HAVE TAKEN CARE OF YOUR FIRST EXCUSE AND understand why (and how) God has prepared you for what He is calling you to do, let's put to bed any further excuses and unpack why you are exactly the person God wants to use.

To do so, let's go back to the story of Moses at the burning bush in Exodus 3–4. Remember, God has called Moses to go to Pharaoh to tell him he'd be taking the Hebrew people out of Egypt and leading them to the promised land. This was a huge calling where God would make good on the promise He made to Abraham four hundred years prior. And God wanted Moses to be "the guy" to do this. But Moses had every reason to tell God why he was not that guy. Maybe you can relate. Maybe you are giving God these same reasons.

In chapter 1, we looked at the first question (or excuse) Moses asked God, "Why me?" What we see is that God prepared Moses through his upbringing. He placed a burden on him through his experiences. And he never disqualified Moses despite the mistakes he made. God made it clear that Moses was the guy for the job. Yet Moses had four more excuses or questions. Let's look at these in more detail.

WHO ARE YOU?

Moses asked God in Exodus 3:13, "If I come to the people of Israel and say to them, 'The God of your fathers has sent me to you,' and they ask me, 'What is his name?' what shall I say to them?" He was asking, "Who are You, God?" and God responded, "I AM WHO I AM" (v. 14). God told Moses, "Say this to the people of Israel: 'I AM has sent me to you'" (v. 14).

Now, if you read this like me, you probably hear something like this from Moses:

"Hey, God, um . . . You want me to go talk to the religious leaders, the elders of the nation of Israel. These guys have seen some stuff, they've done some stuff, and they're experienced sages. These are like the Yodas—filled with wisdom—and You want me to just roll up to them and be like, 'Hey, what's up y'all? My name is Moses. I know we haven't met yet, but God sent me to tell Pharaoh, "Let My people go," and set two million people free from the bondage of slavery.' And when they ask me, 'Who sent you?' You want me to tell them, 'I AM WHO I AM sent me.' I don't know how well that'll work, God, especially since I'm still trying to figure out who You are."

Moses was asking God to explain who He is and how he could present that to the religious leaders in a believable way. He was asking God to give him some proof.

Isn't that what we want too? For God to somehow prove Himself to us, as if He hasn't done that time and time again. But when God calls us to something big, we want to know, "God, who are You?" In other words, "God, why should I believe that You really want to use me to live out this calling for my life?"

God answered Moses, and us for that matter, with three beautiful truths.

1. "I Am . . . a God of Unlimited Power"

When God said to Moses in Exodus 3:14, "I AM WHO I AM" and to tell the Israelites, "I AM has sent me to you," He was showing His unlimited power. He didn't need to say more or explain Himself, because "I AM" says it all. Far too often I find myself wanting God to prove Himself again and again and again, as if all the evidence He gives us from His Word and throughout our lives is not enough. "You want me to do something else, God? Give me more proof."

My friend, you serve a God of unlimited power. Who is He? He can do far greater things than anything you can imagine. You don't have to explain yourself to others. If God sends you, He will take care of the explanation.

2. "I Am . . . One Who Uses Ordinary People"

Because God has unlimited power, He can do extraordinary things with very ordinary people. We think of Moses as a famous biblical character. But before he was obedient to God, he was an ordinary guy.

Understand something here: Pharaoh did not set two million people free because Moses said so but because *God* said so. Moses was the vessel. What God wants to accomplish in and through you is not because of you. It's because of Him. You have an opportunity to be part of something very special. You have an opportunity to do some very incredible things. But remember along the way, we are simply ordinary people who God can use to do extraordinary things. It is still all about Him.

3. "I Am . . . Going to Do the Supernatural"

When we are available and obedient, God does things beyond our wildest imagination. Exodus 3:17 says, "I promise that I will bring you up out of the affliction of Egypt to . . . a land flowing with milk and honey." God used Moses to fulfill a promise He made four hundred years earlier. When you choose to trust the unlimited power of God, He can do the supernatural, even with an ordinary person.

Who are You, God? He tells us, "I AM WHO I AM."

WHAT IF?

Now we get to the third excuse, the third question Moses had for God. After receiving answers to "Why me?" and "Who are You?" Moses still had more objections. Maybe you can relate. This time Moses wanted to play out the classic what-if scenario. In Exodus 4:1 Moses said, "But behold, they will not believe me or listen to my voice, for they will say, 'The LORD did not appear to you.'" Moses was asking God, "What if they don't believe me?"

Maybe you have found yourself asking this same question. *What if I am not good enough? What if they leave me? What if I fail in front of everyone? What if I lose it all?* We are all prone to ask the classic what-if questions. In these instances, I want you to understand something: When we entertain the worst-case scenarios, we are choosing to place our faith in uncertain outcomes rather than in the One who controls those outcomes.

Craig Groeschel, senior pastor of Life.Church, aptly says,

"What you worry about the most reveals where you trust God the least."[1] When you sit deep in thought about what could happen, you give all your attention to the wrong thing. Instead, fix your eyes on the One who controls what will actually happen. Trust that if God calls you to it, He will bring you through it.

God remained patient with Moses and responded to his question by telling him to throw his staff to the ground. When he did, it turned into a snake. Then he picked up the snake by the tail, and it turned back into a staff. God gave Moses two more signs to prove that He had sent him; He told Moses to show the people these signs so they would believe. God gave Moses a mission. When Moses questioned God with, "What if they don't believe me?" God already had it mapped out. He had not one but three signs for Moses to show the Egyptians.

My friend, while you plan out the worst-case scenarios in your head, God already has plans A, B, and C mapped out for you. If He brings you to it, He will bring you through it.

I CAN'T!

Even after three excuses, Moses was still not done. He still wasn't convinced he was the guy for the job. This time, he pointed to his past and his lack of ability. How often do we do the same thing? We hear God's calling and immediately disqualify ourselves because of our past failures or present limitations.

Moses did exactly that in Exodus 4:10 when he said, "Oh, my Lord, I am not eloquent, either in the past or since you have spoken to your servant, but I am slow of speech and of tongue." See, Moses had a speech impediment. He believed that his limitation would keep him from being able to do the job God called him to do. He objected to God's command because he couldn't speak eloquently.

After this fourth objection, God answered Moses' question with a question of His own (something God did often throughout Scripture). He said, "Who has made man's mouth? Who makes him mute, or deaf, or seeing, or blind? Is it not I, the LORD? Now therefore go, and I will be with your mouth and teach you what you shall speak" (vv. 11–12). God responded with confidence in Moses because God was the One who made his mouth.

Maybe you have the same objection. Maybe God has called you to do something you believe is beyond your ability. Maybe you need a qualification or skill set you don't have. But who made you? Who walks with you? With God, we never have to say, "I can't." Philippians 4:13 famously reminds us, "I can do all things through him who strengthens me." God also reminds us in 2 Corinthians 12:9, "My grace is sufficient for you, for my power is made perfect in [your] weakness."

God does not and will not call you where His grace cannot sustain you. Oftentimes God leads us to places where we would fall short on our own. But because of His unlimited power and endless ability, "I can't" turns into "I can!" With God, your shortcomings never have been and never will be your story.

Think about that for a second. For someone who couldn't speak correctly to go to Pharaoh and pull two million people out of Egypt, then lead them into God's destiny, he needed the ability to speak more than a few words. Moses was able to do it because when he couldn't, God could. There are things God is calling you to do that you may be trying to cancel because of what you perceive as impossible. But it's only impossible when you see it through your own strength. Today, God is asking you, *Who made your mouth?*

That deficiency you believe you have, that lack of skill or ability you constantly point out in yourself, who gave that to you? Won't that same God provide everything you need when He calls you and leads you into His purposes?

ON YOUR OWN, YOU CAN'T. BUT GOD CAN.

On your own, you can't. But God can.

THEY'RE BETTER!

Even after all this—after God told Moses why he was the exact guy for the job, after telling him "I AM" sent him, after giving him plans A, B, and C for his what-if scenarios, and even after reminding him that the mouth he struggled to speak from was made by God—Moses still had one more objection. He believed God would be better served by asking someone else. Exodus 4:13 says, "Oh, my Lord, please send someone else." Moses believed there were better people for the job.

Aren't we too often our own worst critic? We seem to find the best in others and the worst in ourselves. We see what they have, how beautiful they are, how much money they have, how they seem to have it all together. But we immediately discredit the blessings God has given us. We go right to our deficiencies. We look at every reason in the world why it can't be us. Why it shouldn't be us.

But see this today: God picked you. When He calls you, He isn't giving you someone else's assignment. It's your mission. Your background brings you to the foreground. Everything that has happened to you, for you, and through you has led you to this place where God has chosen you!

In the Old Testament, Samuel was looking for one of Jesse's seven sons to become the next king of Israel. He considered several of the older sons, the ones Jesse believed were better suited to be king. But God told Samuel those "better" choices weren't His choice. David was (1 Samuel 16:1–13).

Isaiah 55:8–9 reminds us, "For my thoughts are not your thoughts, neither are your ways my ways, declares the LORD. For as the heavens are higher than the earth, so are my ways higher than your ways and my thoughts than your thoughts."

Moses clearly wanted God to choose someone else. And far too often, don't we want the same thing? We look for every reason in the world not to say, "Yes, God, I am the guy." I did it almost nine years ago when I was called to be the pastor of Community Bible Church (CBC).

In 2015, Pastor Robert Emmitt, the founding pastor, called me and said, "Ed, God told me to tell you that you're supposed to be the pastor of CBC." I remember it so vividly.

I said, "Pastor Robert, I'm humbled, but are you joking right now? Because this feels like a joke." He told me he was not kidding. He said God gave him a word, and he had written in his Bible, "Send Ed Newton to be the pastor of CBC." So he called me and told me, "Ed, God told me to tell you that you're the guy."

In that moment, I did exactly what Moses did. I disqualified myself. I told Robert I didn't know how to do that. I told him I had never been a lead pastor before. Like the *Pastor* pastor. Like *the* guy.

But Robert insisted, "Yeah, God told me to tell you you're the guy."

Like Moses, I rejected his call again. I said, "I think you need to tell God I'm not the guy." Robert simply continued to reassure me that I was.

What calling has God led you to? When has God told you you're the guy? Now, this isn't just for men, but you understand my point. You can have all the objections in the world. But when God calls you "the guy," you're the guy.

It's time to stop rejecting His plans. There is no excuse or question that is outside of God's control. God has prepared you for this. He will provide you with unlimited power and do extraordinary things through your ordinary self. Where you are weak, He is strong. My friend, there is no one better for this job. If God has called you, you are the guy!

CHAPTER 3

OVERLOOKED, BUT NOT UNNOTICED

YOU HAVE PROBABLY HEARD THE FAMOUS PHRASE "STICKS AND stones may break my bones, but words will never hurt me." The reality is, this maxim is nothing more than a lie from the devil himself. Not only do words hurt, oftentimes they hurt more than sticks and stones.

As human beings, we are all subject to labels. It seems we receive them from nearly everyone, everyplace we go. Just think about the way you describe people. When you tell one friend about another, you immediately place labels on that person. They are tall or short, athletic or unathletic, smart or not very smart (to put it nicely); maybe you describe them as rich or poor.

Unfortunately, sometimes we are labeled by something we did once. It is not how we want or deserve to be labeled, but in that moment, we are labeled based on something we have no control over.

Make no mistake about it, labels we give and receive are not just descriptions. Right now, you can probably think of four to five, maybe many more, labels that have been placed on you.

These come in the form of things people have said about you, groups you have been associated with, or failures you have been known for. Often they are like stickers we wear around, like the first day of school when you have to wear a sticker or tag with your name on it to learn your classmates' names.

Sadly, far too many people still wear these "stickers" across their chests. Only eventually it's not just in school but everywhere they go. Perhaps you are crippled by the labels you have been given, and you have come to believe those labels define you. If that is you, I want you to know something. The labels put on you were never intended to stick.

Today, they come off.

You no longer have to walk around wearing those labels, even ones you have placed on yourself. God never intended you to tie your identity to a label.

There is freedom from these labels, today. And you must break free from them to believe you are the person God wants to use (and you are).

Before we dive deeper into this, I want to clarify something. Choosing to believe you are the person God wants to use to do something incredibly special is not about self-confidence. The confidence you can have in knowing God wants to do amazing things in and through you is not about you; it's about Him. It is a God-confidence, and it is God-confidence that gives us the self-confidence that can set us free from the labels others have placed on us.

TOO SMALL, TOO WEAK, TOO YOUNG

Do you know that David was labeled too? That's right, King David, whose bloodline included Jesus. The same King David God said was a man after His own heart. And he wasn't labeled by just anyone; he was labeled by his own father.

Let's start from the beginning. You might know the story. It's pretty popular, but I want you to see the details and how even David, someone God used in incredible ways, was labeled from the start.

There was a guy named Samuel, a prophet, who had been given the task of choosing the next king of Israel. The existing king, Saul, was not aging out. God actually took His hand off him when he began to dabble in some of the wrong things.

So the Spirit of God led Samuel to the house of Jesse. Samuel believed that the next king of Israel would be one of Jesse's sons. When Samuel arrived, seven of the eight sons were present. They were lined up oldest to youngest, tallest to shortest. Samuel was ready with oil to anoint the next king (a tradition at that time). First, Samuel came to Eliab, Jesse's oldest son. Samuel thought that surely he was the one God would choose; he was so sure, he had already taken the lid off the anointing oil. Then, 1 Samuel 16:7 tells us, "The LORD said to Samuel, 'Do not look on his appearance or the height of his stature, because I have rejected him. For the LORD sees not as man sees: man looks on the outward appearance, but the LORD looks on the heart.'"

Why was Samuel ready to anoint Eliab? Because he was head and shoulders taller than everybody else. It is the same reason the nation of Israel picked Saul to be king. Isn't it interesting that society defines excellence, success, and prosperity based on height, looks, and the external?

God told Samuel the same thing He tells us now: that we have to look on the inside because the label on the outside might not truly reflect who a person is. Sometimes we are prone to assign the wrong labels. This is why it is so important to reject labels that are contrary to what God has said about you. If you are not careful, you might miss your calling by listening to the lies others have wrongly spoken over you.

Now back to the story. After God told Samuel that Eliab was not His choice to be the next king, Samuel continued down the line of sons. He considered the next son, Abinadab. But God said no. He moved to the next son and the next: "No." Seven sons, and God said no to each one.

At this point, Samuel asked Jesse if he had any more sons. Now, how did Samuel know Jesse had eight sons? Did he stalk him online before making the trip to Bethlehem? God was telling him, "Your future king, yeah, he's not here. Somebody is missing." Jesse responded, "There remains yet the youngest, but behold, he is keeping the sheep" (v. 11). So Samuel told Jesse to send for him. Why would God bring Samuel to a man's house to anoint the next king, only for Him to say no seven times?

The king would come from Jesse's family. But the son He had labeled wasn't there. The next verse tells us Jesse "sent and brought him in. Now he was ruddy and had beautiful eyes and was handsome. And the LORD said, 'Arise, anoint him, for this is he'" (v. 12).

David was *overlooked* but not *unnoticed*.

In this story, David's own father looked at him and basically said, "You're not invited, you don't count, you don't have experience, and you don't have the look." Jesse thought David had some gaps, so much so that when Samuel came to choose a king, he didn't even invite him to be considered. And David had other labels. He was the youngest son. Too small. Too weak. Too young. The one tending the sheep. Certainly he wasn't God's choice to be the next king.

David was discounted because of the labels his father placed on him. Labels like these may have been placed upon us by others, or maybe we have placed them on ourselves:

You're Not Invited

God had an incredible journey lined up for David, and from the jump, he was not invited.

Maybe you can relate. Maybe you applied for a job but didn't get it. Maybe you positioned yourself for an opportunity, but they chose someone else. Maybe the people you tried to get "on the inside" with continue to leave you out, and you feel like you are not invited.

Make no mistake, you have not missed what God has for you. If He has allowed anything to be kept from you, it is because He has even bigger plans in store. Sometimes God will keep us from what seems "good" because He has "better" in the waiting. When others overlook you, God notices you. And He is preparing you for something greater than you can imagine.

You Don't Count

Jesse had counted David out because he was too small, too weak, and too young. Though God was going to choose David,

Jesse labeled him before Samuel even met him, assuming he wouldn't be the God choice. It is so important not to own the labels others have placed upon you, because they can count you out even when God has already counted you in.

AND HE IS PREPARING YOU FOR SOMETHING GREATER THAN YOU CAN IMAGINE.

God used David to take down Goliath, something no other man could do. God used David to conquer Jerusalem, to defeat the Philistines, to build an empire, and to start construction on the first temple. God used David to be the king of all Israel.

Let me ask you something: Would God have used David to do these historically great things if he believed the labels placed upon him? Would David have faced Goliath if he believed he was too small and too weak? Would he have become king if he had believed he was too young and inexperienced?

We know the stories of King David because he did not buy into the labels placed on him. He did not believe the lie that he was counted out. Neither should you. Others might count you out, but God wants to tell you, *You're in!* What He has in store for you might be historically great. But you have to rip the tag off your chest if you are going to step into God's mighty plan for your life.

You Don't Have Experience

Jesse discounted David by saying, "There remains yet the youngest, but behold, he is keeping the sheep" (1 Samuel 16:11). Did you catch that? Jesse essentially said, "Yes, I have another son, the youngest, but he is just a shepherd." Translation: *He doesn't have the experience needed to be the king. He isn't a warrior like my oldest sons.* Yet another label Jesse had placed on David. So he was not invited. He didn't count. He didn't have the experience. Isn't it amazing how we try to qualify people for the jobs God has called them to?

If you are a believer, maybe you have heard by now that God doesn't call the qualified, He qualifies the called. Others can place all the labels they want on you. They can have their own opinions about whether you are the right person for the job. They can try to decide if your résumé qualifies you. But none of that means jack squat when it comes to the plans of God.

Remember, God isn't looking at your ability but your availability. Don't let your lack of experience or age keep you from His call. He has big plans in store for you. And whatever He has called you to, He will lead you through.

You Don't Have the Look

1 Samuel 16:12 says, "And he sent and brought [David] in. Now he was ruddy."

Ruddy. That is the word used to describe how David looked. Many believe this means he was redheaded, and maybe even had reddish cheeks. In other words, he didn't have the look of a king. Even Samuel thought the oldest son would be chosen because of his height. So here is David, redheaded, small, short. Yet God chose Him anyway.

If you are someone who has struggled with your self-image and thought to yourself, *I don't have the right look*, I want you to understand what the Spirit told Samuel about David. "Do not look on his appearance or on the height of his stature, because I have rejected him. For the LORD sees not as man sees: man looks on the outward appearance, but the LORD looks on the heart" (1 Samuel 16:7).

God isn't looking for someone who has "the look," as we often do. That label means nothing to Him. He made you to look exactly as He wanted, and that will not hinder the incredible journey He wants to lead you on.

RECOGNIZE YOUR VALUE

I once read the story of a father who gave his watch to his son. I'll paraphrase it for you here: The watch was priceless, and the father knew it. He wanted the son to understand the significance of the watch's value, so he wanted him to hear what other people would say about it.

The father told him, "Son, I'm giving you this watch, and I want you to go down to the pawnshop, the jewelry shop, and the museum. Meet with the man at the museum who appraises the value of antiques. He's really knowledgeable and will help. Just tell him I sent you."

So the son took the watch and went to the pawnshop. Even though the watch didn't work, and it was a little banged up, he asked, "Sir, how much would you give me for this watch?" The pawnshop owner replied, "Well, I'd give you $10; it's scratched up and it doesn't work." The son said, "Okay," and he went to the jewelry store. There, the gentleman behind the counter said, "I'll give you $100 for it."

Finally, the boy went to the curator at the museum, a friend of his father's. The son laid the watch down for him to examine. As he looked at the watch, the curator began to speak. "This watch, even though it doesn't work and is beaten up, is about two hundred years old. I'd say it's worth $300,000."

The son returned to his father and asked, "Dad, you knew what this watch was worth, didn't you?"

The father responded, "Sure did, son. If you aren't careful, you'll listen to people who put a price tag on you, ones who do not recognize your value, and you'll actually discount yourself. So don't stay long in places or with people who minimize you to feel better about themselves. Surround yourself with those who see the worth in who you are and better yet, whose you are."[1]

My friend, don't allow the labels placed on you to discount who you are and, more importantly, whose you are. God used David to do things we talk about to this day. But first, he had to look past the labels and recognize his own value. He may have been overlooked by his earthly father, but he wasn't unnoticed by his heavenly Father. Neither are you. You may have been labeled. You may have been overlooked. But you are not unnoticed. God is going to use someone to do something incredible. Why Not You?

CHAPTER 4

ANOINTED, BUT NOT YET APPOINTED

OKAY, MAYBE BY NOW YOU HAVE BOUGHT INTO THE IDEA OF "WHY Not You?" You believe God has called you to something greater for your life. Now what? The calling is clear: You might know what He is "going" to do. You might even know "where" He is leading you. So why hasn't it happened already? He called you; shouldn't He swoop you up on a magic carpet and take you there?

Not exactly. There is a part of David's story that gets overlooked. After Samuel anointed him as the next king of Israel, do you know what David did? He went right back to the pasture to shepherd his sheep. That's right. He didn't go to the palace right away. He had a job to do.

Though he was anointed, he was not yet appointed. You may not be where you want to be yet, but that does not mean God has not appointed you for something, somewhere, at some time. Until that point, your job is to rest in the anointing He has for you, right where you are.

SOMETIMES YOU HAVE TO BE FAITHFUL IN THE SMALL THINGS, THE SECRET THINGS, AND THE SACRED THINGS BEFORE HE APPOINTS YOU TO THE GREAT THINGS HE WANTS TO DO IN AND THROUGH YOU.

Now you might be asking, *Why?* Why doesn't God appoint us the second He anoints us? Sometimes you have to be faithful in the small things, the secret things, and the sacred things before He appoints you to the great things He wants to do in and through you.

God often won't give you more if you aren't faithfully stewarding what you already have. There are some who say, "If God would just give me more _____, *then* I would be a good steward." But what evidence is there of that? Why would God believe you would be a different steward with more than you are with little?

He's clear about this in Luke 16:10–11. "One who is faithful in a very little is also faithful in much, and one who is dishonest in a very little is also dishonest in much. If then you have not been faithful in the unrighteous wealth, who will entrust to you the true riches?" God has already given us the answers to the test. If you want Him to hand over the keys to the kingdom, you must first prove that He can trust you with the shed out back.

So how do we do this? What does it look like to be anointed but not yet appointed? God wants us to prove we are faithful in three key areas before He appoints us.

1. The Small Things: God wants to know you are serious about the small things He has placed under you before He entrusts you with more. God put David over a pasture before He gave him the kingdom of Israel.
2. The Secret Things: God wants to know you are a person of integrity who will do what's right even when no one is watching. David protected his sheep in the wilderness with no one else around.

3. The Sacred Things: God wants you to worship, praise, and seek Him on your own, not just on Sunday mornings. David learned to worship in isolation. He was the singing shepherd.

God wants to see that our faithfulness is consistent. Because even when others aren't watching, He always is. Whether He has put you in a place around thousands of people or without a single soul in sight, He wants you to be a person of excellence in everything you do. Being faithful in the small, secret, and sacred things is what prepares you for the big things God wants to do in your life.

Throughout this book, you are going to see that God wants to use you to do incredibly special things. But before He can trust you to do the spectacular things, He wants to know He can trust you to do the incredibly normal, everyday things He has for you. That is what David showed of himself, and God allowed him to be exalted and used in much, much bigger ways.

When David was not yet appointed, King Saul needed comfort from a tormenting spirit (1 Samuel 16:14). No one seemed able to help him until one of his servants said, "I know a guy." He said to King Saul, "Behold, I have seen a son of Jesse the Bethlehemite, who is skillful in playing, a man of valor, a man of war, prudent in speech, and a man of good presence, and the LORD is with him" (v. 18). At this time, David was not even fifteen years old, and here is someone saying, "Let me tell you what I see in him."

- He's skillful.
- He's a man of valor.
- He's a man of war.
- He's prudent in speech.
- He's a man of good presence.
- He's a man whom God is within.

David, who according to his father was not invited, didn't count, didn't have the experience, and didn't look the part, was "the guy" Saul's servant believed could help him. Don't miss this: Because David was faithful in the small things, God rewarded him in much bigger ways.

And God didn't stop there. One day in the midst of war, David's father wanted him to be the errand boy for his brothers at ground zero, on the front lines. David had recently been anointed king. You could probably still smell the fragrance of oil on his body. 1 Samuel 17:17–18 says, "And Jesse said to David his son, 'Take for your brothers an ephah of this parched grain, and these ten loaves, and carry them quickly to the camp to your brothers. Also take these ten cheeses to the commander of their thousand. See if your brothers are well, and bring some token from them.'"

David came rolling into the battleground with some Hot-N-Ready five-dollar Little Caesar's pizzas (I took interpretive liberty here) for his brothers, who were at war versus the Philistine giant, Goliath. What David saw when he got to the battleground was that this giant was blaspheming his God and the nation of Israel while the Israelites stood around in fear. None of them wanted any part of facing him. But David asked some of the soldiers about the reward for killing Goliath. They responded by telling him the conqueror would get rich, marry the king's daughter, and no longer pay taxes (1 Samuel 17:25–27).

David's brother was not happy. "Now Eliab his eldest brother heard when he spoke to the men. And Eliab's anger was kindled against David, and he said, 'Why have you come down? And with whom have you left those few sheep in the wilderness? I know your presumption and the evil of your heart, for you have come down to see the battle'" (17:28).

What was Eliab doing? Placing labels on David. He was saying, "What are you doing here? Go back to your little sheepfold; this is a battle for soldiers, not a little kid."

David rejected Eliab's label, asking others, "Hey guys, what's in it for the person who beats Goliath?" As in, "What's the prize?" They repeated the reward, and David was like, "Bet."

When Saul heard about David's boldness, he called for David. Now, Saul should have been the one to fight Goliath, the one leading his troops with military strategy. Yet for forty days and forty nights, the mighty men of Israel were paralyzed with fear. That is, until a fifteen-year-old boy with a stack of five-dollar pizzas walked up and said, "I'll take that guy. Let me have a swing at him" (vv. 31–32, my paraphrase).

In response to David's request, Saul labeled him. "You are not able to go against this Philistine to fight with him, for you are but a youth, and he has been a man of war from his youth" (v. 33).

Once again, David rejected the labels, basically saying,

"No, no, no, Saul. The God who delivered me from the mouth of the lion and the bear when I was caring for the sheep will deliver me from the giant" (vv. 36–37, my paraphrase). Saul had to decide what to do, because David was the only one who wanted to step into the octagon against Goliath.

For David to battle Goliath, he needed armor. So Saul offered David his own armor. "Then Saul clothed David with his armor. He put a helmet of bronze on his head and clothed him with a coat of mail, and David strapped his sword over his armor. And he tried in vain to go, for he had not tested them. Then David said to Saul, 'I cannot go with these, for I have not tested them.' So David put them off" (vv. 38–39).

I believe the last five words of verse 39 are so important as we talk about the labels we carry: "So David put them off." The armor symbolizes labels that Saul tried to put on David. Saul was saying, "David, if you are going to defeat the giant, you have to look like this, have this, do this, use this." Why did Saul want to give David his armor? Because if David defeated Goliath, Saul would have gotten the glory. He could have said, "I gave him my stuff."

Understand this: You can't face your giant wearing someone else's armor.

When you feel inadequate or insecure, you may think, *If I had their looks, their intelligence, their bubbly personality, their athleticism, their connections, their job, their financial situation, I could do what God is calling me to.*

But here's the thing: Their anointing

> YOU CAN'T FACE YOUR GIANT WEARING SOMEONE ELSE'S ARMOR.

and giftings weren't made for you. Perhaps their armor is too small for what God has called you to do. Avoid looking at what others have. Their armor is for their battles. Trust that God will give you exactly what you need for yours.

A CHAMPION, NOT A CONTESTANT

In the sports world we hear this story of David versus Goliath as a representation of the big team versus the small team, or really, the big team versus the underdog. But understand this: David is not the underdog. Goliath is. Why? Because God is not on Goliath's side.

See, when God is on your side, it doesn't matter the size, the stature, the situation, or how we perceive things. When God is on our side, who can be against us?

It was not like David was trying out to be a contestant that faced Goliath. He was a champion, chosen by God. So where did David get this confidence? It was not a self-confidence; it was a God-confidence. He was anointed to be a king, and God would lead him there.

CHOSEN BY GOD

My wife and I have been watching the TV show *Madam Secretary*, which came out in 2014. Madam Secretary, whose name in the show is Elizabeth McCord, becomes president in season six (spoiler). However, even though I knew that detail of the plot, while we were watching season five, I was questioning whether she would make it out of the current episode.

Elizabeth is in a meeting when the building gets rocketed by some grenade launchers, then the show ends. It's the ultimate cliffhanger.[1] Have you ever been left hanging when a TV show ends? You don't really have time to watch the next episode, but you watch the first five minutes of it to make sure the character lives. Well, that's what I did. And it turns out she survived.

And then it dawned on me. Every time I watch this show, I see the opening credits for *Madam Secretary*, and her face is in it. She wouldn't die in season four if her face is in the opening credits. She'd make it to the end. For all six seasons and all 120 episodes, she would be the face of the show.

David's season four included his encounter with Goliath. He wasn't going to die, because in season six he'd be the king. So he walked in this confidence, going, "God, You chose me; therefore, no matter what I face, I will walk in God-confidence. Whatever giant I fight, I will prevail over, not by my power but by Yours. You have called me to something greater, and this is just a stop on the way to the palace."

CULTIVATING A CRAFT

I think sometimes we tell this story wrong; we act like David went to Toys"R"Us, got a little wrist-rocket with a couple of marbles, popped Goliath in the head, and won. The end. What gets missed in this story is that David was a slinger.

If you've never read this in the Bible, some people were slingers, also known as snipers. What David did is the equivalent of taking a long rifle into a sword fight, but he was not the underdog, because God was on his side. While he was alone in the pasture being faithful in the small things, the secret things, and the sacred things, he was cultivating a craft. This wasn't some measly BB gun he was shooting at cans. This was actually defending his sheep in a real way, like a long-range sniper.

David was never going to lose to Goliath. He wasn't the underdog. He was chosen by God, cultivating his craft while in the pasture leading his sheep. What God has prepared you for should assure you that you are not an underdog with the odds stacked against you. When you are obedient to God's call for your life, He will make you a champion. He will prepare you so that when the time is right, you will be appointed.

God has a special appointment designed for *only you*. What do you do while you are anointed (knowing God is going to use you for a specific purpose) but not appointed (to the place or position He is leading you to)? You continue to cultivate your craft, knowing God has chosen you. To truly believe this reality, you must shed the labels others have placed on you.

There is a story called *You Are Special* by Max Lucado.[2] The book follows a character named Punchinello, who is a wooden character called a Wemmick. These Wemmicks were made by a master craftsman named Eli. Punchinello lives in

Wemmickville, where every Wemmick receives either gold stars or gray dots. The stars are for when they do something good, and the dots are for when they do something bad.

Punchinello was covered with gray dots. He was not fast enough, smart enough, or quick enough; he was simply not enough. But one day, he met a girl with no stickers. No gold stars, no gray dots. Punchinello was curious.

He asked the girl why she had no stickers. She told him to see Eli because he was the maker of all the Wemmicks. So Punchinello went to Eli and asked, "Why don't the stickers stay on her?" Eli responded softly, "Because she has decided that what I think is more important than what they think. The stickers only stick if you let them."

Punchinello didn't understand. "What?"

Eli explained, "The stickers only stick if they matter to you. The more you trust my love, the less you care about their stickers." When we choose to stop caring about the stickers, they will fall off.

If you want to be appointed to what God has anointed you for, it's time to let the stickers fall off. David became king because though he was overlooked and labeled, he knew he was noticed by God. Though he was not yet appointed, God had anointed him. And because God had appointed him, when he faced his greatest battle against Goliath, he was not simply a contestant but would come out a champion.

You are noticed. You are appointed. You are a champion. But if you are going to step into the calling God has for you, it's time to shed the labels.

CHAPTER 5

STOP LIVING THE LIE

AS CHRISTIANS, WE ARE PRONE TO CHARACTERIZE OUR BATTLES as good versus evil. Of course, this is easy for us to process. It is how we make sense of the narratives in our heads. Like the shows or movies we watch, we tend to think of battles as angels versus demons.

And there is truth to this. When you think about the eternal battles we face, there is a real devil. There are real demons who seek to destroy you, not just to inconvenience you but to end you, not just to thwart the plans God has in store for you but to take you out, not just to frustrate you but to nullify your impact and influence.

But sometimes the battles we face are internal battles— not of good and evil, but over what God has said about you, and whether or not you will choose to believe Him. If you're like me, sometimes you are your own worst enemy. I often do more damage to myself than the devil does. As a result, I often choose not to believe what God believes about me.

If you struggle with the same problem, I want you to understand something: Choosing to believe what God says about you is not arrogance. As with David, the goal is not self-confidence but God-confidence. You must realize that God has you appointed, chosen, and destined for a specific purpose.

Embrace this today: The position of success God has

given you and the fact that you made the team, got the job, landed the deal, built something, or created a legacy is not because of happenstance or circumstance. It is not just good luck or good karma.

> YOU MUST REALIZE THAT GOD HAS YOU APPOINTED, CHOSEN, AND DESTINED FOR A SPECIFIC PURPOSE.

God has positioned you. God has given you a platform. God has allowed you to prosper. God has put you in a specific place. Don't doubt what He has spoken over you. We have a tendency to not believe what God has said about us. Second Corinthians 10:4–5 says, "For the weapons of our warfare are not of the flesh but have divine power to destroy strongholds. We destroy arguments and every lofty opinion raised against the knowledge of God, and take every thought captive to obey Christ."

Your identity is at risk when you choose to believe that your worth is predicated upon your acceptance and accomplishments. When your value is inextricably connected to the ever-changing situations and circumstances around you, you will find yourself on a roller coaster of emotions, up and down, based on how things are going.

There is a concrete reality God wants to speak over you today: Your life is meaningful. Your life is significant. You are not evolutionary matter, made up of some catalytic collision of chemical components. God formed you and fashioned you in your mother's womb before you were a twinkle in your daddy's eye, long before you were a conversation between two people who loved each other. Before the positive pregnancy test, God was positive about you. He predetermined your steps and organized your way. He has spoken over you. The question is: Will you receive what He has put in motion in your life?

God did not make a mistake when He made you. When the Bible says we must tear down every lofty opinion, that includes the inner critic and the inner dialogue that says, *I'm not enough. I don't do enough. I'm not good enough. I don't have enough.*

Let God Almighty speak over you: *You are enough.* It's time to stop living the lie, and believe that today.

As you read this book, I want you to remember that you are already chosen, already worthy, already enough. Let the doubts and the insecurities go. This is your time. Be confident in who God says you are and the value you bring. What is happening is not by accident. You have been prepared for this moment.

IMPOSTER SYNDROME

Even though God has told us we are enough and has called us to a special purpose, we still feel fake at times—that we'll be exposed, and our place, position, and prosperity will be taken from us. This equates to something called *imposter syndrome.* We all experience it in our lives, and if you are going to be used by God, it is something you are going to have to overcome.

The sentiment of imposter syndrome is the disconnect between the responsibility or status you have been given and your internal dialogue about how you are perceived. In other words, you may find yourself elevated in title or responsibility, yet you have self-talk and fear similar to this: *What if people find out I'm not really who they think I am?*

A MASK NOT MADE FOR YOU

Before LED or IMAX screens, ancient Greeks found entertainment in theater plays. These plays were often viewed in large auditoriums seating up to ten thousand people. Because of this, it was difficult for people in the upper levels to clearly see facial expressions of the actors or actresses and know what was happening.

Remember, they didn't have any type of screen projecting a closer view of the thespians. So instead, they used larger-than-life masks, held up on sticks. The masks displayed the emotion the play meant to convey in any given scene. As the scenes changed, the masks changed.

This is how the people in the upper levels knew what was going on. But get this, at this time in history, they did not call the performers *actors* or *actresses*; they called them *hypocrites*. Now, we see this word as a negative term, but it means "two-faced." They called the performers this because, throughout the play, they would hold up multiple masks or faces, if you will.

How many of us wear multiple masks in our own lives, based on where we are, who we are with, or what the "vibe" is in a given moment? You walk around in your own skin, yet you end up trying to live in someone else's. You become someone you don't believe you are. But don't miss this: When you try to be like someone else, you are telling God, "You made a mistake."

God didn't mess up when He made you. He didn't make you to be a version of someone else. He made you to be the original you. God hasn't called you to be a person who wears multiple masks. He wants you to be the you He made you to be. Because at the end of the day, that will always be enough.

ACCEPTANCE BASED ON PERFORMANCE

Sometimes we are a product of our own environments. When our parents or someone we look up to has the tendency to be controlling or show us acceptance based on performance, we internally shift our mindset. We think, *In order for me to be loved, I have to follow certain rules,* or *I have to perform to a certain level.*

Even in social statuses or social media, we see what is applauded and what is rejected. Thus, we become internally hardwired to think, *I want to be accepted, so I have to fit in.* We start to grab multiple masks, all the while becoming the hypocrite.

If you struggle with imposter syndrome, you are not the only one. You are actually in good company. Albert Einstein wrestled with imposter syndrome, saying that he thought of himself as an involuntary swindler.[1] I wonder if he was completely overwhelmed by people considering him to be the most brilliant man on earth. If he were anything like me, perhaps he thought the day would come when he would be exposed.

He wasn't the only famous person to struggle with imposter syndrome. Tom Hanks faced the same struggle and at one point said, "No matter what we've done, there comes a point where you think, 'How did I get here? And when are they going to discover, that in fact, I'm a fraud and take everything away from me?'"[2]

Barbara Corcoran, the real estate agent and mogul who is a regular on the hit show *Shark Tank*, said, "Who doesn't suffer from imposter syndrome? Even when I sold my business for $66 Million, I felt like an absolute fraud!"[3]

You are not the only person to deal with imposter syndrome. But you can't let it keep you down.

THE SIGNS OF IMPOSTER SYNDROME

If you are wondering whether you struggle with imposter syndrome, let me ask you a few questions. It should be noted these are indicators, not indictments.

- Do you mistrust the compliments people give you?
- Do you feel unworthy of success?
- Do you feel persistent self-doubt?
- Do you underestimate your contribution?

- Do you criticize yourself even after others give you praise?
- Do you have a fear of being exposed?

I encourage you not to rush through these questions but to actually sit and think through your answers. If the answer is yes to any of these questions, why do you think that is? If you answer yes to any of these questions, this serves as a friendly nudge to be aware that oftentimes we are our own worst critic.

We struggle with these questions because of how we perceive ourselves. And that perception often reflects the small view we have of ourselves and of God. So as you think through these questions, I want you to know that God is saying, *I will never give up on you. I will never grow tired of you. Your past has no claim on you. I will put a robe of righteousness on you. I am not disgusted by you. I will fight your battles for you. Numerous are My thoughts toward you. I sing over you. I chose you. I fully know you. I fully love you.*

How do I know He is saying these things to and about you? Because He says so in His Word! All of these are statements God has said about you in Scripture.

Your value is not tethered to your accomplishments, the possessions you have, or what other people say about you. You do not have to try harder or do better.

Have you ever gotten something you spent a long time pursuing? Maybe you saved up and bought it. Maybe you worked really hard and obtained it. You chased after that one element, thinking, *I'll feel complete satisfaction the moment I get _____.*

But then you realize you didn't find that satisfaction.

You can have a bigger house and still not have a home.

You can have a nicer car and still feel like you are living in poverty.

Nothing on this planet can give you what you've been looking for except the God who made you. Your value is bigger than a logo or a brand. It is not predicated upon trophies, certificates, or applause. Far too often we find ourselves hoping that if we could "do this" or "get that," it would be enough. But when will we realize that anything and everything we chase in this world will never be enough?

In 2005, Tom Brady sat down for an interview with Steve Kroft on *60 Minutes*. In it, Brady said, "There are times where I'm not the person that I want to be. Why do I have three Super Bowl rings and still think there's something greater out there for me? I mean, maybe a lot of people would say, 'Hey man, this is what is.'

"I reached my goal, my dream, for my life. Me, I think: 'God, it's gotta be more than this. I mean this can't be what it's all cracked up to be. I mean, I've done it. I'm twenty-seven. And what else is there for me?'"[4]

The interviewer followed up Brady's statement with a question: "What's the answer?"

Brady responded, "I wish I knew."

The things of this world were never meant to fulfill you. What you are chasing—more accolades, more praise, more acceptance—will never be enough. If you continue to chase the world, you will continue to be empty, wondering like Brady, *What else is there for me?*

C. S. Lewis made a great point when he said, "If I find in myself a desire which no experience in this world can satisfy, the most probable explanation is that I was made for another world."[5] God made us to walk with Him. He is our provider and supplier. He is the One who gives us our worth.

Before we move on, I want to press in on three questions:

1. *What are you afraid of losing?* What would you lose if others learned the truth about you? What would they see if you took off the mask? Is it worth hiding behind an identity that was never meant to be yours?

2. *What are you trying to hide?* Is it worth all the effort you are putting in, just so others don't see the real you? Why do you struggle with their opinions and standards if God has told you that you are enough?

3. *What are you trying to prove?* How far will you go to prove something God hasn't asked you to prove? When will you decide to finally rest in the identity Christ gave you and settle into the comforting truth that who you are is enough? God doesn't need you to prove anything. Just be you.

It's time to stop living a lie. The things you are afraid to lose, that you are trying to hide, or are still trying to prove are the things keeping you from becoming who God created you to be. God's going to use somebody, so why can't it be you? But He can't use you until you decide to stop living the lie. It's time to take off the mask and believe what the God who created you says about you: You are enough.

CHAPTER 6

YOU ARE NOT
AN IMPOSTER

IF YOU ARE STILL READING THIS BOOK, IT TELLS ME YOU BELIEVE
God wants to use you in ways beyond your imagination. But before you can own that belief and step into the life and calling God has in store for you, you must overcome imposter syndrome because it is holding you back.

Quick reminder, imposter syndrome is when we fail to believe the undeniable truths God has said about us, despite all the evidence to prove it. It can show up in a number of ways, and even nonbelievers struggle with imposter syndrome. It is when, despite the promotions, successes, awards, achievements, goals obtained, and recognition, we still feel like a fraud.

It's as if we are living in fear that somebody, at some point, is going to find out we are not who everyone else believes we are. In the last chapter, we looked at the sentiment and signs of imposter syndrome. Now let's look at the symptoms, struggles, and scriptures against it, along with strategies to overcome it.

THE SYMPTOMS OF IMPOSTER SYNDROME

When we feel like an imposter or fraud, our underlying low self-view leads to a small view of God, pushing us to prove ourselves to please or pacify people. Often when we step into a position of significance, success, or leadership, we hear statements like, "Fake it till you make it." But if you feel fake and you don't feel like you are going to make it, you will live in perpetual fear, which shows up in one of two ways: (1) You try to outperform everyone else around you (to prove yourself or please people), or (2) you don't want to step forward, so you recommend somebody else due to self-sabotage or fear of failure (to pacify).

Let me be very clear. Both are wrong. Ian Simkins, lead pastor at The Bridge Church in Nashville, Tennessee, says, "You live out what you believe about yourself whether it's true or not."[1]

Pete Scazzero, author and founder of New Life Fellowship in Queens, New York, puts it this way: "The vast majority of us go to our graves without knowing who we are. We unconsciously live someone else's life, or at least someone else's expectations for us. This does violence to ourselves, our relationship with God, and ultimately to others."[2]

Let me tell you, I know exactly what Pete is saying because that was me when I became the pastor of CBC. When I was first called to this role, I started wearing suits every day. Now, that wasn't the norm for me; I wasn't used to rolling up in a suit. Growing up, I was a basketball player and a skateboarder. Those two things heavily dictated my fashion sense.

But when you don't view yourself the way God views you, you dress in a certain way, hoping people will respect you. That was my story.

At that time in my life, my value was tethered to whether people came to our church. So you can imagine how tough it was for me when I walked into the church hallway one day and a brother pointed in my face (with his wife and four kids behind him), saying, "We'll give you one more week to prove yourself." Or in a leadership meeting (on three different occasions) when an individual looked at me and said, "Jury's still out on you, Newton." It was really hard. But these are perfect examples of why it's unwise to place your value in trying to prove, please, or pacify others.

I am grateful that in the moments of criticism, God was patient as I grabbed a figurative mask (or suit and tie) to cover up my insecurities. As I struggled with the feeling of being a fraud, Pastor Robert reminded me in private, "Ed, God brought you here. God chose you. God actually spoke to me and said you're the guy. Stop caring what other people think and stop trying to fill my shoes."

Pastor Robert Emmitt's impact and leadership in San Antonio placed him in the same conversation as iconic figures like Gregg Popovich, head coach of the five-time NBA champion San Antonio Spurs. Man, I felt some pressure as his successor. But Pastor Robert told me, as only he could, "Don't fill my shoes. I'm taking mine with me. You gotta bring your own shoes."

So I kicked off those dress shoes and I put my Jordans back on. And for the first time in a long time, I was comfortable in my own skin again.

Don't fall victim to imposter syndrome. It's time to stop

trying to perform well to gain acceptance or to pacify people by putting others forward in an effort at humility, when in reality, it is just your insecurities speaking.

If God put you in that place, He has equipped you and He has qualified you. You may not be the expert, but nobody's asked you to be. You may not be perfect, but nobody's asked you to be. Embrace it. If God felt you were worthy enough for the title or role, then you are. Period.

> **IF GOD FELT YOU WERE WORTHY ENOUGH FOR THE TITLE OR ROLE, THEN YOU ARE.**

THE STRUGGLE OF IMPOSTER SYNDROME

Paul told us something very important in Ephesians 5:15–17: "Look carefully then how you walk, not as unwise but as wise, making the best use of the time, because the days are evil. Therefore do not be foolish, but understand what the will of the Lord is."

In other words, Paul was saying to stop living for other people and instead seek to live out the will of God. Don't wait for applause, living for everyone else's acceptance while dying from their rejection. That's the definition of living unwise, as Paul put it.

I know that sounds harsh, but if we are going to talk about the struggles that come with imposter syndrome, we must be brutally honest. That means if you don't choose to believe what God says about you, but instead believe the lies of the Enemy,

- your true identity will never be actualized,
- your calling will never be realized,
- your gifts won't be maximized, and
- your impact and influence will be minimized.

When you and I don't live in our kingdom purpose, we miss out on finding our true identity, the calling God has for our lives, how we could use the gifts He's given us, and impacting and influencing others in ways beyond what we would believe is possible.

The God you serve could change your situation in the snap of a finger. He is a God who walked out of the grave. A God who says nothing is impossible for those who believe in Jesus. That same God is telling you, *I have called you to do great things.* If we don't embrace what God has chosen us for, we will miss the very reason why we are on this earth. God is going to use somebody. Why Not You? God is going to bless somebody. Why Not You?

And yet we feel like an imposter, saying, "God, can't you pick somebody else?"

In His patience, not giving up on us, He still says, "No, I chose you."

You might be saying, "Ed, this sounds like self-help." It's not. This is about finding your identity in Christ Jesus. Galatians 2:20 challenges us: "I have been crucified with Christ. It is no longer I who live, but Christ who lives in me. And the life I now live in the flesh I live by faith in the Son of God, who loved me and gave himself for me."

THE SCRIPTURES AGAINST IMPOSTER SYNDROME

I want to say something that should free up someone who is reading this right now: Did you know that you do not have to do anything for God to accept you? That's right, you don't have to win an award, get that promotion, get married, be top of your class, go to college, have kids, drive a nice car, be popular, or make six figures. *You don't have to do any of that; God still accepts you.*

"Behold, a voice from heaven said, 'This is my beloved Son, with whom I am well pleased'" (Matthew 3:17). When God spoke about Jesus, His Son, in Matthew 3, Jesus had done nothing well-known up to that point. He hadn't fed the five thousand with five loaves of bread and two fish. He hadn't walked on water. He hadn't performed a single miracle. Yet before He did anything significant, God said He was *well pleased* with Jesus. Jesus had done nothing, and His Father still accepted Him.

You know what? He feels the same way about you. Jesus teaches us that in in Him, you are enough. You are accepted. You are chosen. You have been destined. You are beloved. We know all of this because Scripture tells us so. Let's look at what Christ specifically said that will help us wipe away the feeling of being an imposter.

Your Identity Is in Christ

When we have the right frame of mind and see our identity in Christ, it frees us to realize we are not tied to the labels others give us or the accomplishments we have achieved. Philippians 3:7 says, "But whatever gain I had, I counted as loss for the sake of Christ." Paul was saying that no gain came from all his worldly accomplishments compared to living out Jesus' purpose for his life. As it says in Matthew 16:26, "For what will it profit a man if he gains the whole world and forfeits his soul?" The reason you and I struggle with imposter syndrome is because we have attached our identity to trophies and titles rather than to Christ.

You are not a fraud. But you are also not a CEO, CFO, athlete, artist, five-time award winner, chef, ten-time champion, or three-time teacher of the year. These are activities and accolades you may have been recognized for. They are not your identity. Don't want to be an imposter? Find your identity in Christ.

You're His Workmanship

Not only is your identity found in Christ, but He made you to be exactly who you are! Ephesians 2:10 says, "For we are his workmanship, created in Christ Jesus for good works, which God prepared beforehand, that we should walk in them."

How do you separate yourself from imposter syndrome? Be you. It sounds simple because it is. Now, just because it is simple does not make it easy. Those are two different things. Being yourself is simple in concept but can be difficult to carry out. That means in every setting, in every group of people you are around, whether at church, the ballpark, school, the office, at home, or out at dinner, you are the same person. You are who God created you to be. You do not have to wear different masks, because you were made in God's workmanship to be exactly who you are.

Your Weakness Does Not Disqualify You

Earlier we learned that the labels, mistakes, and weaknesses you have do not disqualify you from God using you in incredible ways. Paul reminded us of this in 2 Corinthians 12:9: "But [the Lord] said to me, 'My grace is sufficient for you, for my power is made perfect in weakness.' Therefore I will boast all the more gladly of my weaknesses, so that the power of Christ may rest upon me."

Paul, a man God used to do incredible things, experienced weakness himself. The Bible doesn't specify what this weakness was, but it was bad enough that Paul begged God (on multiple occasions) to take it away. But God essentially told him, "You know what, Paul, I don't need to take it away. Because in your weakness, My power will shine through you."

Do you know why this is important? Because when we do incredible things for God despite our weaknesses, it reveals His power. On our own, our weaknesses would limit us from achieving what He has called us to do. But your weakness doesn't disqualify you. God will do special things in and through you, and His power will be perfected wherever you are weak. Don't miss the unimaginable things God wants to do in your life because you have weaknesses. Guess what?

> **DON'T MISS THE UNIMAGINABLE THINGS GOD WANTS TO DO IN YOUR LIFE BECAUSE YOU HAVE WEAKNESSES.**

Every person (besides Jesus) who ever lived had weaknesses. God hasn't disqualified you, so don't disqualify yourself!

You're in God's Providence

Do you know why you do not have to fear being a fraud or an imposter? Because God has predestined you, called you, justified you, and glorified you. Romans 8:29–30 says, "For those whom he foreknew he also predestined to be conformed to the image of his Son, in order that he might be the firstborn among many brothers. And those whom he predestined he also called, and those whom he called he also justified, and those whom he justified he also glorified."

Let me ask you a few questions. How could you be an imposter when your identity is found in the One who created you rather than in the labels you wear and the accomplishments you gain? How could you be a fraud when God created you to be exactly as you are? How could you be an imposter when the weaknesses you display don't disqualify you but only magnify what God can do in and through your life? How can you be a fraud when God has already predestined you, called you, justified you, and glorified you?

These aren't just truths I'm saying about you. God's Word makes it very clear that these things are true of you.

Breaking free from the feelings and thoughts of imposter syndrome may come down to this one challenge: Will you choose to believe your negative emotions and self-talk, or will you choose to believe what God has said about you and predestined for you before you ever took your first breath?

STRATEGIES TO OVERCOME IMPOSTER SYNDROME

Now that we have looked at Scripture and we know what God says about us, how do we break free from imposter syndrome to become all God has called us to be?

First, we separate feelings from facts: "We destroy arguments and every lofty opinion raised against the knowledge of God, and take every thought captive to obey Christ" (2 Corinthians 10:5). Your feelings of inadequacy, failure, or being a fraud are not true. Feelings are not fact; they just reflect our emotions in a given moment. Feelings change, but facts stay the same. We just went through multiple passages of Scripture that tell us the facts about who God says we are. If you want to overcome imposter syndrome, it starts with choosing to believe God's truth over your feelings.

Second, stop self-sabotaging and accept praise: God will put people in your life to encourage you and push you toward His purpose for your life. It is all part of His grand scheme. But when He puts these people in your life, you can't reject their encouragement; they were sent by Him. Why is it that we can receive one hundred compliments and one criticism, and we stay stuck on the one critique? God has not called you to fix your mind on the negative. When He sends people to encourage and praise you, accept it. Allow God to encourage you through others.

Third, embrace failure and grow from it. Henry Ford's great quote notes, "Failure is only the opportunity more intelligently to begin again."[3] Stop deflecting opportunities to step into God's calling, suggesting with false humility that God use someone else. He has chosen you. He's called you.

Finally, avoid the "fake it till you make it" trap. Rather than running from God's call, *face it* till you make it, head-on, and know He is with you every step of the way. Paul challenged us in 1 Timothy 6:12 to "fight the good fight of the faith. Take hold of the eternal life to which you were called and about which you made the good confession in the presence of many witnesses."

Is the feeling of being an imposter keeping you from stepping into God's calling for your life? Do you find yourself trying to prove, please, or pacify people? Do you struggle with your identity, basing who you are on the acceptance of others through what you have accomplished?

It's time to put down the masks. God is telling you today you are His. Your identity is in Him. You are His workmanship, made exactly as He desired. Your weaknesses do not disqualify you but allow you to be the one He uses to exemplify His glory.

He predestined you. He called you. He justified you. And He glorified you. It's time to separate your feelings from the facts. Stop self-sabotaging and accept the praise He puts in front of you. Embrace failure and use it to grow into who God is calling you to be.

Victory isn't about believing in your achievements and skills. It is about recognizing who you are and what you have in Jesus Christ. You are *not* an imposter. You are a child of God, and He is preparing to use you in unimaginable ways.

CHAPTER 7

THE PIT OF REJECTION

I HOPE YOU ARE BEGINNING TO SEE THAT GOD WANTS TO USE you to do some incredible things. As I have said, God is going to bless somebody. God is going to use somebody. God is going to destine somebody to do great things for Him.

The question I want to continue to put at the forefront of your mind is, Why Not You?

If you choose to take that step of faith and believe that you are the person God wants to use in incredible ways, there is something you need to understand: Your current reality is not your final destination.

> YOUR CURRENT REALITY IS NOT YOUR FINAL DESTINATION.

Here's why this is important to understand: You have a God who has put a dream in your heart. That means regardless of your age, you can embrace the fact that if you are alive, a God dream is living inside you, and that dream isn't about you. God is choosing to use you as the answer to someone else's problem. The very thing somebody is waiting on, looking for, or anticipating, God can do through you. The God dream given to you might be the answer to what is going on in another person around you.

But you cannot help others until you step into God's dream and pursue it the way He intended. God wants to break off the misconstrued ideas you have about yourself: the insecurities, the insufficiencies, and the inadequacies; the labels you have placed upon yourself or allowed others to place upon you that have kept you from stepping into God's dream for your life.

It's time to dream again. You must embrace the dreams God has given you. Good dreams go unfulfilled. But God's dreams cannot be stopped.

To steal the title of the Green Day song, right now some of you are living on the "Boulevard of Broken Dreams"[1] because you think your current reality is your final destination. But what I want you to embrace today is that God's dreams cannot be stopped. If He set a dream in motion, there is nothing any man, any group of people, or any plot can do to stop or hinder His ultimate purpose in it.

A guy named Joseph had a God dream. His story starts in Genesis 37. Maybe you've heard of him. He is a pretty popular biblical character who, because he remained faithful to God, lived out the dream inside him, one so significant Scripture recorded it and we still discuss it to this day.

See, Joseph had this really cool coat, otherwise known as "the coat of many colors."

It wasn't a Louis Vuitton coat but a multicolored coat given to him by his father. Genesis 37:3–4 tells the story. "Now Israel [Jacob] loved Joseph more than any other of his sons, because he was the son of his old age. And he made him a robe of many colors. But when his brothers saw that their father loved him more than all his brothers, they hated him and could not speak peacefully to him."

Joseph's dad, Jacob, had two wives. They were sisters. (Yeah, and you thought the Bible was boring.) Sidenote: If you were putting together a book of God with all the stories, wouldn't you want to tell only the good stories? God doesn't do that, though; interestingly, the Bible doesn't hide the bad stories. It talks about a perfect God who used some pretty jacked-up people. But it does so to help us understand that He takes broken pieces on the Boulevard of Broken Dreams and turns them into masterpieces.

Okay, back to our story. I don't want to go into too much detail, but the drive-by version is that Jacob had two wives who were sisters: Leah, the oldest sister, who Jacob was deceived into marrying, and Rachel, the younger sister, who was the woman he truly loved. Jacob did not want to marry Leah but was deceived by his future father-in-law, who gave the older sister in marriage after seven years of earning his trust. Jacob had to work another seven years (a total of fourteen years) to earn the favor of his father-in-law and get the girl he really wanted.

Joseph was special to Jacob because he was the firstborn of Rachel, the woman who Jacob wanted. Originally, she was unable to have children, while Leah, the older sister, was very fruitful.

Rachel was jealous of Leah and gave Jacob permission to sleep with the maidservants so he could have sons with them. So he was not only sleeping with his two wives but also hooking up with two maidservants. When Rachel finally conceived, she had Joseph, then later Benjamin, the twelfth son. Jacob had twelve sons total, the other six with Leah and four from his maidservants.

Do you see why Joseph was the favorite? Joseph was treated as an only child. Through no fault of his own, his brothers resented him for it. Then add the coat. It was significant in that, according to archaeologists, it extended down to Joseph's wrists, exempting him from work.[2] So you already had jealous brothers; then they saw their younger brother was given a special coat, and that coat has exempted him from working. Not very cool in the eyes of the brothers.

Then Joseph took it a step further. He decided to tell his brothers about his God dreams. About the first dream he basically said, "I had a dream from God that the eleven sheaves (that's y'all) bow down to me." By the way, when you share dreams like this with your brothers, who already hate you, you can't expect it to go over very well.

But Joseph continued with his second dream, saying he saw the sun, the moon, and eleven stars bowing down to him. At that moment, "they hated him even more for his dreams and for his words. . . . And his brothers were jealous of him, but his father kept the saying in mind" (Genesis 37:8, 11).

I don't know the context of how Joseph shared this in sentiment and emotion, but maybe you can relate. Perhaps you have sent a text message, and it ended up having a whole lot more emotion attached to it than you originally intended. Sometimes others can attach emotions to our words that we don't necessarily intend; it's just how our words are perceived. We don't know if Joseph just rolled up to his brothers and went, "Umm, guys, I had a dream. You all are going to serve me. God told me to tell you this is how it'll go down."

But I can tell you this: Bishop T. D. Jakes said it best in a sermon years ago: "Be careful who you tell your dream to."[3]

Because Joseph shared his dreams with the wrong people, they had every intention of ruining and even ending his dreams. "They [his brothers] saw him from afar, and before he came near to them they conspired against him to kill him. They said to one another, 'Here comes this dreamer. Come now, let us kill him and throw him into one of the pits. Then we will say that a fierce animal has devoured him, and we will see what will become of his dreams'" (Genesis 37:18–20).

They did not end up killing him, but they did take off his coat and throw him in a pit with no water source. They left him there to die. The Bible also says they sat there and ate lunch while he was screaming. Pretty cold-blooded, wasn't it? Later they went back to their father, Jacob, with the coat dipped in blood to show that Joseph was dead.

In reality, they were hoping everything about Joseph, including his dreams, would die in that pit. But the dreams didn't die. Instead, they began to come to fruition. Remember, good dreams aren't always fulfilled, but God dreams cannot be stopped.

THREE TYPES OF PEOPLE

For Joseph, the pit was part of the story. God used the pit and what his brothers meant for harm for Joseph's good. There is an important lesson here. You must be careful who you share your dreams with. Maybe you're reading this book and you have given up on your dream because you told the wrong person and allowed them to influence your pursuit of that dream.

In that same sermon from Bishop T. D. Jakes, he said something that really stuck with me, and I want to paraphrase it for you: You've got to be wise about who you invite into the sacred space of your calling. Not everyone is equipped or anointed to carry the weight of your dream. If we're not discerning, we'll end up sharing God's vision for our lives with people who misunderstand it, mislabel us, and may even work against us. And let's be honest, some folks don't just walk away from your dream; they try to shut it down.

That hit me hard. Bishop Jakes went on to talk about the three types of people in your life: confidants, constituents, and comrades.[4] As you read the following descriptions, think about who is walking with you now. And as you walk out the calling God has placed on your life, be prayerful about who you keep or let into the room.

1. *Confidants*—These are your people, the ones who are with you not because of what you do or where you're going but because of who you are. They don't flinch at your flaws, and they don't define you by your worst decisions. They celebrate your wins and sit with you in the losses. They remind you of who you are in Christ when you forget. These people are rare, but they are a gift—your inner circle, your people.

2. *Constituents*—These folks roll with you, but only

because you're headed in the same direction. You're aligned on mission, for now. But be careful, the moment your vision shifts or God calls you to something they don't understand or agree with, they'll bounce. They were never really for you; they were for what you stood for. Don't get it twisted. These aren't the ones you share your God dream with.

3. *Comrades*—Now these are the people who link arms with you, not because they love your vision but because they dislike the same things you do. It's unity over a common enemy, not a common heart. They might fight beside you for a season, but when the battle changes, they disappear. They're not loyal to you; they're loyal to the fight.

Share your God dreams only with your confidants. You might be saying, "Ed, I have only one or two confidants based on your description." If that is the case, God bless you, because many people don't have a single one in their lives.

Now, I hope that if you are married, the first person that comes to mind is your spouse. Your husband or wife should be the one person you can share any God dream with, and nothing will be too crazy or out of the realm of possibility because they support you and help your God dream become a reality in any way possible. That is a confidant.

Whether you are sharing your dream with your spouse, colleague, significant other, classmate, or coworker, this should be a person that you not only seek counsel from but a person you can share your dreams with.

These people, when you tell them your God dreams, are not threatened by you but will figure out how they can encourage you, enable you, and equip you to do all God has called you to do. They are not jealous of you, and they do not want your favor or connections to your success, because they know God has a specific plan and purpose for them too. They pursue their God dreams while fully supporting yours. They want to walk with you in your giftings and cheer you on. You often discover confidants when you are obedient to God's calling and He brings success upon your life. You will find out who will stand in your corner based on how they act around you.

It is important that you only share your God dreams with confidants and never share them with constituents and comrades. Constituents and comrades will likely take you down the Boulevard of Broken Dreams, and if you are not careful, they will convince you to give up on the God dream you are destined to live out. Maybe you were daring to dream again, and something happened. You got pushed into a pit. You faced a form of rejection, a challenge, slander, or gossip. You faced a situation, and you didn't walk into the pit but were pushed into the pit because someone was jealous or envious of you and tried to stop your dream. And you gave up on your dream because it was not received the way you thought it should be.

Listen, people will be quick to tell you dreams can't come

true. But just because they don't add up doesn't mean God isn't in them. We serve a God with a different math. He adds by multiplying, and He divides by subtracting. If Jesus can roll back the stone, walk out of the grave, and say He's defeated sin, death, and hell, He is able to do the miraculous and supernatural in and through you.

Comrades are united by what they're against, not what they're for. Let's break this down with a little Texas flavor. Think of Houston and Dallas, two cities with very different vibes. Houston is all about hustle, diversity, and that gritty, industrial energy. Dallas is buttoned-up, business savvy, and proud of its polished, corporate culture. They don't really have a lot in common. They may even talk about each other with a little shade.

"Dallas is too bougie."

"Houston's too chaotic."

But you know what brings them together? They both can't stand Austin.

They'll unite real quick to roll their eyes at Austin's traffic, weirdness, or how it thinks it's the center of the universe. So now they're suddenly friends. They're liking each other's tweets, reposting memes, cracking jokes because they have a common enemy.

But the truth is, that "friendship" only lasts as long as Austin is in the conversation. Once Austin leaves the group chat, Houston and Dallas go back to their normal rivalry. That's what comrades are like: They link arms with you, but not because they believe in your dream or even understand you. Comrades are just riding with you because you both dislike the same thing.

But hear this loud and clear: Just because someone hates what you hate doesn't mean they love what you love. You can't trust them with your God dream because once the conflict ends, so does the connection.

Constituents are people who are with you as long as you stand for what they stand for. They appear loyal, but their loyalty is not to you—it's to the cause or stance you currently share. The moment your stance shifts or the cause changes, so does their support.

Imagine a coworker who champions you because you're both advocating for the same policy change at work. They stand with you, support your emails, nod in every meeting. But once leadership implements that change and you shift your focus to advocating for better health benefits (something they don't prioritize), suddenly they're silent, distant, maybe even oppositional.

They weren't for you; they were for what you were standing for. And once that aligned mission ended, so did their support. Constituents make it seem like they're with you, but they're really with the agenda.

Your God dream may require you to pivot or stand for things that challenge comfort zones. Constituents won't follow you through that evolution. And if you entrust them with something sacred, they may abandon or even oppose you when the dream leads somewhere they're not willing to go.

DON'T GIVE UP

Don't give up on your dreams just because you ended up in the pit of rejection.

What if I told you your dreams could be resurrected in a pit? Joseph was sold into slavery from that pit. Now that might sound negative and I'm sure Joseph wasn't thrilled about it at the time, but he didn't know that with every moment God was bringing him closer and closer to the dream He gave him. This is why you cannot judge your current situation as your final destination. It is a stop on the journey necessary for where God is taking you. Asking, Why Not You? begins with recognizing God has given you dreams. Although you don't understand how it all will work, and even if your current reality doesn't match up with what He's been telling you, choose to trust Him in the process.

You can't microwave your current situation. Trust that while you wait, God is working on your behalf. Just because you find yourself in the pit of rejection, it is not your final chapter.

You might have been mistreated or misunderstood, but don't give up on the God dream inside you. Dare to dream again. The pit you are in is only a stop on your way to the incredible mountaintops God will lead you to.

CHAPTER 8

THE PIT, THE PLACE, AND THE PRISON

NO MATTER WHO YOU ARE, WHERE YOU COME FROM, OR WHAT YOUR past looks like, you were made for a purpose. Not only that, but God has placed God dreams inside you that you are destined to live out. Unfortunately, as we discussed in the last chapter, many people are living on the Boulevard of Broken Dreams; they've tucked theirs away.

Many of us resonate with this. We have decided not to pursue our dreams and therefore miss the purpose God made us for. Why do we do that? Because we allow the pit, the place, and the prison to defeat us rather than propel us into our God-designed destiny.

In the last chapter we talked about the pit of rejection. Joseph, who was highly favored by his father, was given two God dreams. The dreams said that one day his eleven brothers would bow down to him. His brothers rejected the dream, rejected Joseph, threw him into a pit, and planned to leave him there to die.

But what his brothers meant for evil, God meant for good. The pit of rejection was just the first step on Joseph's way to living out his God dream. That pit was not the last obstacle he would face. The place of accusation and the prison of the forgotten awaited him before he realized his destiny.

THE PLACE OF ACCUSATION

After being thrown into the pit, things were not looking promising for Joseph. His brothers ultimately decided to sell him into slavery for twenty pieces of silver. You might be asking, "Ed, why that specific amount?" At that time in history, that was the same price of a handicapped slave.

So his brothers not only threw him into a pit, but they sold him at a discounted rate. Can I tell you something today? You aren't discounted. Your dream isn't dashed. God's resurrecting a dream in you that He gave you. You've faced some obstacles, you've faced some challenges, and you might have quit and given up, but God has used everything in your life to get you where you are and will keep on using it to take you where you are going.

After being sold into slavery, Joseph ended up in Egypt at the house of Potiphar. Potiphar was second-in-command to Pharaoh (the king of Egypt) as the captain of his guard. We'll pick the story up in Genesis 39:2–4. "The Lord was with Joseph, and he became a successful man, and he was in the house of his Egyptian master. His master saw that the Lord was with him and that the Lord caused all that he did to succeed in his hands. So Joseph found favor in his sight."

Listen, my friend, somebody might have stolen your coat. But they can't steal your anointing. They cannot steal the favor of God on your life. They took something from you. But they did not take the anointing, the favor, the success, or the hand of God off you.

Even though Joseph was thrown into a pit and sold into slavery, God stayed right by his side, granting him success in all that he did. But then things got interesting: Joseph caught the eye of Potiphar's wife. I guess you could say she was the original "desperate housewife." "Now Joseph was handsome in form and appearance. And after a time his master's wife cast her eyes on Joseph and said, 'Lie with me'" (39:6–7).

Now, it's one thing for her to be attracted to Joseph, but in this moment she essentially said, "Hey, Joseph, nobody's watching us. Let's sleep together. No one will ever know."

But Joseph refused her. "How then can I do this great wickedness and sin against God?" (v. 9).

Joseph was flourishing, then he faced temptation. If there was ever a time to throw back at God that he was thrown into a pit, sold into slavery, and brought to this moment, this was it.

But Joseph didn't respond that way. He continued to trust God. He knew his final destiny was not his current reality. God was on the move, and Joseph didn't know exactly how He was working. Joseph could have said, "I am going to live for me. I'm going to fulfill my cravings and my desires. Forget God, nobody's watching." Instead he decided it didn't matter that nobody was watching. It didn't matter that it was just him and Potiphar's wife. He knew God was watching, and God had been too good to him and brought him too far for Joseph to betray Him.

Wait a second, *too good*? Shouldn't it be the opposite? Shouldn't Joseph be mad at God or blaspheming Him? Perhaps, but Joseph chose to bless God and be faithful in a moment of true integrity.

If you want God to bless you and bring your God dreams to fruition, start by being faithful in the small things. If you aren't faithful in the small things, you can't expect God to give you the greater things. He is looking for faithfulness at both ends of the spectrum:

- When Nobody Is Watching: Integrity and character require doing what is right when nobody is watching. The Bible tells us in Luke 16:10, "One who is faithful in a very little is also faithful in much, and one who is dishonest in a very little is also dishonest in much." If you want God to bless you and anoint you ever more, then be honest and do what is right in the small moments when nobody is looking.
- When Everyone Is Watching: When God does give you success and notoriety, do you use that to promote yourself or to serve Him? As you prove you are faithful in the small things, God will begin to bless you in bigger ways. But He doesn't do so for you to turn a spotlight onto yourself. Joseph didn't use his success for personal gain with Potiphar's wife. Instead, he continued to honor God.

Both attitudes are important in realizing your God dreams. Joseph maintained them even when he had no idea where his choices would take him. We must remember, though, that he didn't see the final picture.

It's easy for us to read stories like this and know what decision the main character should make, because we know how the story turns out. We know that if Joseph had chosen wrong, he would have jeopardized the blessings God eventually brought him. We know these blessings because we know the full story. But Joseph didn't . . . just like we don't know *our* full story. Choosing to honor and obey God is just as important in our story as it was in Joseph's.

God had given Joseph dreams. Not "good dreams," because as we looked at in the last chapter, good dreams often go unfulfilled, but God dreams cannot be stopped. Even after his brothers threw him into a pit, God still fulfilled his dreams.

Next, Potiphar's wife tried to sideline Joseph. After he faithfully refused to sleep with her, she continued to tempt Joseph day after day, until one day she ripped off his cloak as he ran from her seductive demands. She then took the cloak to her husband and twisted the story, as if Joseph was trying to tempt *her*. This led Joseph from Potiphar's house to prison, the next step on the journey toward his God dream (Genesis 39:11–20).

THE PRISON OF THE FORGOTTEN

From the pit to the place to the prison, one thing remained: The hand of God was on Joseph as he continued to be highly favored. The guard of the prison placed Joseph, an inmate, in charge of all the inmates (Genesis 39:21–23). It might seem like his situation was on a downward spiral—down, down, down. But actually, we see that Joseph's dreams weren't falling apart; they were falling right into place.

At some point, Pharaoh's cupbearer and baker were thrown into prison. "And he put them in custody in the house of the captain of the guard, in the prison where Joseph was confined. The captain of the guard appointed Joseph to be with them, and he attended them. They continued for some time in custody. And one night they both dreamed—the cupbearer and the baker of the king of Egypt, who were confined in the prison—each his own dream, and each dream with its own interpretation" (Genesis 40:3–5). They had dreams that needed interpretation. Insert Joseph, who revealed that his God could interpret their dreams (vv. 6–8).

After they shared their dreams with Joseph, he very honestly told the cupbearer he would live, and the baker that he would die. Joseph didn't hold back; he spoke the truth. And it all happened exactly as he said (vv. 9–13, 16–22).

Before the cupbearer went back to Pharaoh, Joseph made a request of him. "Only remember me, when it is well with you, and please do me the kindness to mention me to Pharaoh, and so get me out of this house. For I was indeed stolen out of the land of the Hebrews, and here also I have done nothing that they should put me into the pit" (vv. 14–15). "Yet the chief cupbearer did not remember Joseph, but forgot him" (v. 23).

Are you reading this right now and feeling forgotten? Maybe you have a God dream, and you've ended up in a pit. You tried to be faithful in the small things, but life isn't working out the way you thought it would, and now you feel forgotten. In moments like this, you have to take into consideration: What God has in store for you might not be ready yet. On one side, God is working on your destiny, what He has called you to. But it might not be ready yet. Sometimes we have to wait while He is working.

WHAT GOD HAS IN STORE FOR YOU MIGHT NOT BE READY YET.

If you try to shortcut the process God has for you, you could jack it all up. So God protects you from you. He will not allow you to be where you are supposed to be before you are supposed to be there. When it is time, and your call is ready, He will reveal it to you. It is also possible that you are waiting because you are not ready yet. Sometimes God is working on our situation. We are ready, but we have to wait for Him to work in our circumstances. Other times, the circumstances are ready, but you are not. God will not give you what He has for you until you are ready to receive it.

The challenge here is that if what God has for you is ready, but you are not ready, you must seek Him, His plan, and His agenda until you are ready to receive all that He wants to bless you with. In these seasons that God is working on you, there are things God is going to remove from you, things that need to be reprioritized in you, reorganized in you, and repented out of you. He still has to work on you.

Sometimes we are ready, but God needs to work in our circumstances. We see this in Joseph's life after he was forgotten in prison. God removed Joseph as a slave in Potiphar's house and promoted him to head of all Egypt, as Potiphar's superior, second-in-command only to Pharaoh (Genesis 41).

How did this happen? Pharaoh had a dream that needed interpretation. And the cupbearer, who had forgotten Joseph two years earlier, suddenly remembered him. He told Pharaoh, "You need your dream interpreted? I know a guy."

So Pharaoh called for Joseph, pulling him out of prison and asking him to interpret his dream. Joseph did so, warning Pharaoh of a coming famine and sharing exactly how Pharaoh needed to prepare for it. Pharaoh placed a necklace around Joseph, gave him a chariot with spinners, put a royal ring on his finger, and elevated him to second-in-command. Then he told Joseph that everyone would bow to Joseph when they saw him. Crazy. Did he just say people would bow to Joseph? That sounds like God's dream.

That was the moment.

God had prepared Joseph. God had prepared his situation. His destiny was about to unfold.

Before I tell you how the story ended, understand something: God made a promise to Abraham, Isaac, and Jacob (Joseph's dad), saying, "I will multiply your offspring as the stars of heaven and will give to your offspring all these lands. And in your offspring all the nations of the earth shall be blessed" (Genesis 26:4). Abraham didn't see the fulfillment of that promise. Isaac didn't either. Jacob, whose family had grown to seventy people at the time of the famine, knew the disaster could kill all of them. God's promise wasn't looking good for them. In fact, that promise would have died in the desert if Joseph had died in the pit. But God raises up men and women with God dreams because it isn't ultimately about them; it's about God working through them to help others.

Joseph's brothers traveled to Egypt because they heard there was food there. When they arrived, the brothers who threw Joseph in the pit found themselves face-to-face with him, but they didn't recognize their brother. Joseph likely had a shaved head and was braceleted up like the Egyptians.

On their second visit to Egypt, Joseph invited them to a meal in his home. When he couldn't hold in his emotions any longer, fighting back tears, he looked at them and basically said, "It's me. It's me. Your brother." Immediately and out of fear, they begged Joseph not to kill them. But he told them, "What you meant for evil, God meant for good. And He put me here to save your life" (Genesis 50:20, my paraphrase). As Joseph told them all those years ago, the eleven brothers bowed at his feet.

Do you see it? The dream. God's dream.

Joseph was put there to save those who tried to kill him. He wasn't bitter though, because he realized his God dream wasn't about him. It was about God.

Matthew chapter 1 wouldn't exist if not for Joseph's God dream. Sometimes we skip over Matthew 1 because it is just a huge list of names. But at the bottom of that list is Jesus. Abraham, Isaac, Jacob, and the lineage of Jesus are also on that list. Don't miss this: Abraham's line wouldn't make it to Jesus if Joseph hadn't ended up in Egypt.

God wants to use you in ways greater than you could ever

imagine. The dreams you let die on the Boulevard of Broken Dreams aren't dead. Good dreams often go unfulfilled, but God dreams cannot be stopped. They don't die in pits. They don't get derailed in Potiphar's house. And they don't get locked up in some prison. Difficult situations bring a realization and a clarity of the dreams God places inside us.

It's time to fully receive and pursue your God-given destiny and purpose. Do not shortcut His work in your life. Let God continue to work on you, and rest in the fact that He has something greater for you than you could ever create for yourself. He didn't bring you this far to drop you.

Do not grow weary in waiting for Him to set things up. When it all comes together, it will be a beautiful moment, a moment of destiny.

Embrace the dream. Pursue the dream. And know that nothing you face—no pit, no place, and no prison—can stop God's dreams from coming to fruition in your life.

CHAPTER 9

BELIEVE
DIFFERENT

DO YOU KNOW GOD'S WILL FOR YOUR LIFE? IF NOT, NO NEED TO WORRY, the Bible tells us exactly what God's will for us is. "For this is the will of God, your sanctification" (1 Thessalonians 4:3).

Sanctification is the action or process of being freed or purified from sin. God wants us to become more and more like Jesus every day. That is the will of God for your life. By now you know that God is going to use someone to do something great for His kingdom. The question I continue to challenge you with is, Why Not You? If God is going to bless someone and allow them to live out His will for their life, why can't that person be you? We run into problems when we don't see ourselves through God's lens. Sometimes we fail to pursue His purpose for us because our minds are limited by misbeliefs. This is why God wants to redeem our minds, because a redeemed mind leads to a renewed mind. And when you change the way you view things, the things you are viewing change.

So we know the will of God is sanctification. What God wants is for us to become more like Jesus every day. We see all throughout Scripture that God is working to transform our minds, because if He can transform us, He can lead us to think more like He thinks and see more like He sees.

When you receive the Holy Spirit, there is a transformational reality that happens in your life. When you begin to understand how you look at things, the way life looks begins to change. "For as he thinketh in his heart, so is he" (Proverbs 23:7). (A little King James Version for you.)

The mind is a powerful tool. So how will you use it? Will you allow yourself to be controlled by emotions and moods? Or will you choose to believe the facts of the Bible and set your mind on Christ?

Consider the encouragement in Romans 8:1–8:

There is therefore now no condemnation for those who are in Christ Jesus. For the law of the Spirit of life has set you free in Christ Jesus from the law of sin and death. For God has done what the law, weakened by the flesh, could not do. By sending his own Son in the likeness of sinful flesh and for sin, he condemned sin in the flesh, in order that the righteous requirement of law might be fulfilled in us, who walk not according to the flesh but according to the Spirit. For those who live according to the flesh set their minds on the things of the flesh, but those who live according to the Spirit set their minds on the things of the Spirit. For to set the mind on the flesh is death, but to set the mind on the Spirit is life and peace. For the mind that is set on the flesh is hostile to God, for it does not submit to God's law; indeed, it cannot. Those who are in the flesh cannot please God.

Then, Isaiah 26:3 says, "You keep him in perfect peace whose mind is stayed on you, because he trusts in you." To simply summarize Isaiah and Paul, that which we are fixed on becomes the filter through which we live our lives.

Modern psychology teaches what the Bible has been telling us since the beginning of time. That is, what you believe dictates how you behave, and how you behave dictates what you become. Psychologists say that many problems, such as eating disorders, relational challenges, addictions, depression, and anxiety, are rooted in negative patterns of thinking.[1] Everything ties back to our beliefs. That is why it is so important to believe what God says about you, not what you feel in a given moment.

So what do we do when we struggle to believe God's Word over our feelings? Psychology tells us to try behavior modification. But the truth is, change begins with inward transformation. By transforming your heart and mind, you will begin to transform your behavior.

Don't work on the external, hoping it will fix the internal. Work on the internal by the power of the Holy Spirit. And that is the best part: You don't have to do it by yourself! The Holy Spirit will renew and change you.

If you aren't careful, you may begin to think, *I just have to do better*. But simply "doing better" doesn't work. Instead, empty yourself and let the Spirit of God fill you up. This means submitting to Him and His will on a daily basis, walking with a renewed mind.

Let's look at a couple of verses that remind us of the Holy Spirit's power at work in us:

> "Not by might, nor by power, but by my Spirit, says the LORD of hosts."
>
> (ZECHARIAH 4:6)

"But you will receive power when the Holy Spirit has come upon you, and you will be my witnesses in Jerusalem and in all Judea and Samaria, and to the end of the earth."

(ACTS 1:8)

If you want to change your behavior, begin by changing your beliefs. That's where the power rests.

THE POWER OF BELIEF

I was born in Charlotte, North Carolina. During the months of June and July, I spent my summers in a town called Pilot Mountain, where my grandparents lived. As a child, my grandfather made it very clear to me that we only cheered for a few select sports teams, no matter what. As long as I was living in his house, we cheered for these teams. One was the Atlanta Braves. You might remember at 7:05 p.m. on TBS, every night, a baseball game aired. And they usually featured the Braves. They were my team because that was my grandfather's team.

However, the Braves weren't his only team. From the time I was in the second grade, my grandfather taught me, "Son, we cheer for Duke in this house." Now, at the time I didn't know one of the greatest basketball rivalries of all time would turn out to be North Carolina versus Duke. I just cheered for Duke because my grandfather told me to cheer for them.

What I came to notice was that finding acceptance and joining in the camaraderie led me to cheer for the same team as my grandfather. When you are cheering for something together and seeing the wins and losses deeply affect the person you care about, you recognize that your beliefs are now centered around their acceptance. I didn't want to create any animosity or friction by cheering for a different team.

As a young man I thought, *If my grandfather cheers for Duke, I'll cheer for Duke.* Now here I am at forty-nine, still cheering for Duke. I recently saw someone wearing a royal-blue sweatshirt, no logo or brand attached to it, but I immediately thought to myself, *They must be a Duke fan, wearing that Duke blue.*

WHAT YOU BELIEVE IN SHAPES WHO YOU BECOME. This is a prime example of the power of belief. What you believe in shapes who you become. This is why God places such importance on renewing our minds.

FOUNDATION OF BELIEF

The ideology or set of principles that help you interpret your everyday realities make up the foundation of your beliefs. The Bible refers to this as a biblical worldview. As a Christian or follower of Jesus, you don't put on your biblical-worldview glasses and see through the eyes of Jesus only when you come to church. Yet this is what many people practice.

So often, people have two sets of glasses. They wear their "church glasses" on Sunday mornings, Wednesday nights, and anytime they are around their Christian friends or family.

Then they put on their "worldly glasses" when they go out to dinner, to the bar, the club, or a ball game on the weekends, as if they believe you can separate the two.

When you are set free by the power of Jesus Christ, you get LASIKed. You can't help but see Jesus everywhere you are and in everything you do. He gives you 20/20 vision for His kingdom. As believers and followers of Christ, we are not called to change our glasses based on our location. We should operate with kingdom vision at all times when God has renewed our minds.

FORMATION OF BELIEF

Our experiences, encounters, and environments affect our values, which in turn shape our beliefs. When you look at your neural pathway development (I know I am getting really scientific here, but stay with me), what you see is that your beliefs are shaped by your values. Your values determine how you live in relationship with other people and make everyday decisions. Here's how all this works:

These values and beliefs are being shaped by neurons linking together, creating highways and pathways in your brain for messages to be sent and neurotransmissions to travel these highways.

These pathways develop an "easiness" of processing information, so when we see or experience something repeatedly, we don't have to work that hard to understand or attend to it. Our minds connect the dots based on our experiences, encounters, environments, and education.[2]

For example, you have driven the route you take to church, school, or your office so many times that you can multitask, doing or thinking about something totally unrelated, and still get to your destination without even remembering how you got there. That neural pathway is solidified. However, when something new comes into your life, your mind has to process, catalog, and categorize it to filter the new thing.[3]

FILTERS OF BELIEF

Our cognitive biases become filters through which we process information quickly based on our preferences and experiences. That filter goes back to our experiences, encounters, environments, and education.

Cognitive bias is when you are no longer being objective, which is seeing the truth for what the truth is. Instead, you become subjective. You interpret situations based on how you feel, what you think, or the experiences you had in a given moment.[4]

Let me give you an illustration: One time I was running in my mom and dad's neighborhood in Chipley, Florida. I ended up in the back part of Chipley, out in the country, and I came across a massive dog. This was no ordinary dog; it was a Rottweiler. Based on images of Rottweilers and moments when I had encountered them up close and personal, I think they are pretty intimidating dogs.

This Rottweiler jumped off the porch and started to run after me, not to greet me but apparently to devour me. I ran as fast as I possibly could; I think I could have passed Forrest Gump and Usain Bolt both. I jumped across the street, not even bothering to look both ways. I just hoped the dog wouldn't follow. Sure enough, it stopped on the other side of the road.

My heart was beating a million miles a minute. From that moment, a neural pathway developed in my mind based on that experience. To this day, I am very afraid of dogs whenever I go for a run. Here is how that plays out: When I am running and see a dog, I immediately go to the other side of the street.

Neural pathways can be dangerous, though, if we don't properly process our experiences. I could create a cognitive bias that all dogs are bad. This could even be played out on a more severe level: All dogs must die, or I die.

You might be asking, "Ed, how did you get to that conclusion?" If we are not careful, we will play out our cognitive biases based purely on our own negative experiences. And those experiences become the filter through which we see things.

You might have trauma of your own, experiences you avoid or places you don't go because of what you felt in those spaces; things you avoid smelling because the moment you smell them, something is triggered inside you; things people say that immediately bring you back to a traumatic time.

Trauma rewires our minds, and we don't even know it. Then we stop living to the fullness of what God has called us to. Our experiences paralyze us and create cognitive biases in our minds. Our beliefs filter through our cognitive biases, then they direct how we behave, and how we behave influences who we become. We live in fear. We live as victims rather than the people God created us to be.

Christianity comes into a divine collision with these cognitive biases when we have faith and belief in the God who can renew our minds, no matter what we have been through. Romans 12:2 commands us, "Do not be conformed to this world, but be transformed by the renewal of your mind, that by testing you may discern what is the will of God, what is good and acceptable and perfect."

So how do we embark on this journey of a renewed mind? The answer is not to "try harder" or "do better" but to rely on the Holy Spirit.

You may ask, "Ed, you actually believe that God can renew your mind?" Absolutely He can. God can heal and renew your mind no matter what beliefs and neural pathways have been established. God's character is good. He can be trusted. His ways are always right, and His provision is sufficient in your life.

God didn't plan for you to experience trauma. God is not the cause of your trauma. But He will redeem and rectify it. He will somehow use the scars of your experiences, and His redemptive work in your life will become a story you can use to impact others. But in order to experience this redemption and healing, you are going to have to renew your mind. What you put in your mind must be different if you are going to see yourself the way God sees you. Let God make a masterpiece of your broken pieces. Allow God to renew your mind.

CHAPTER 10

BREAK YOUR PATTERNS

ONCE, A YOUNG GIRL WAS FLYING ON AN AIRPLANE THAT WAS experiencing tremendous turbulence. When the plane settled, adults sitting next to this girl noticed she appeared to be an unaccompanied minor. They looked over to her and asked, "Child, how did you remain so calm in the midst of that violent turbulence?"

The girl's response says it all. She said, "'Cause my daddy's the pilot, and he's taking me home."[1]

The girl had no fear of the outside circumstances because she trusted the one flying the plane. It's a beautiful illustration of the trust a child has in her father. The question is, in the midst of the turbulence in your life, do you have that type of trust in your heavenly Father? Are you able to remain calm despite life's most difficult storms?

Joseph Prince said this: "The devil wants to disturb your mind, trouble your heart, and agitate your emotions."[2] He is skilled at turning our attention off God (the pilot) and onto our emotions (the turbulence).

But 2 Timothy 1:7 encourages us. "For God gave us a spirit not of fear but of power and love and self-control." The truth is, God gave us everything we need to overcome the negative emotions and circumstances in our lives. But to do so, we have to break our patterns.

This requires a perspective change, to believe that no matter how much turbulence you feel and no matter how hard life gets, you can trust God because He's the pilot. Take your mind off your current circumstances and the emotions tied to them, and place them on the One in control of all things. You feel no fear because He is the one leading the way.

No matter the highs or lows, God sees what we can't. He reminds us in Isaiah 55:8–9, "For my thoughts are not your thoughts, neither are your ways my ways. . . . For as the heavens are higher than the earth, so are my ways higher than your ways and my thoughts than your thoughts." Our viewpoint will always be limited compared to God's.

Our perspective is determined by how we process information and respond to it. We all process things through our present realities. These are known as senses: sight, smell, sound, touch, and taste. Sensations move us to our emotions. Then our emotions create feelings, our feelings create behaviors, and our behaviors create outcomes. This means that if we want to change our outcomes, we don't start with behavior (like psychology may tell us to). We start with how we process information through our beliefs. This is why what you believe about God, about yourself, about the people you encounter, and about the things that happen to you are so important. Why? Because they inform your emotions.

One scientific study shows that we have more than thirty-four thousand different emotions. This is because we can experience multiple emotions at the same time. Scientists have shrunk these thirty-four thousand emotions into twenty-seven different categories, but even that list can be reduced to the following eight:[3]

1. Anger
2. Sadness
3. Fear
4. Joy
5. Interest
6. Surprise
7. Disgust
8. Shame

But there is more to consider than just raw emotions. We have to ask, What is the difference between emotions and feelings? The two are often used interchangeably, but are in fact distinctly different.

Emotions are nouns; feelings are verbs. Emotions are chemical reactions within your body, while feelings are the social, cultural, and individual interpretations of those emotions. Circumstances do not determine our emotions; our thoughts and responses toward those circumstances do.[4]

What triggers our thoughts, you ask? Our five senses: sight, smell, sound, touch, and taste. When we experience a situation, it informs our thoughts. Those thoughts create emotions, emotions create feelings, and the feelings create moods.

As we begin to understand how this works scientifically, we need to familiarize ourselves with a fancy term: the *amygdala*. This is an almond-sized structure in the center of your brain that prepares the body for action. It releases adrenaline and cortisol, and it moves us in the direction of fight, flight, or freeze.

The amygdala is responsible for emotions and survival instincts. My amygdala fired as soon as I saw the Rottweiler that I mentioned earlier. I was running. I wasn't going to freeze, and I sure wasn't going to fight.

I want to introduce you to another part of the brain: the hippocampus. This is the learning and memory center that moves short-term information into long-term memory. Based upon a moment or experience, a neural pathway is created that determines how we will process any information we take in that is associated with it. This reaction creates hormones in our body that drive physical processes such as our heart rate and blood pressure. These hormones facilitate communication between the brain and the body, and sometimes we find ourselves slowing down to the point that we can't even make decisions.

Our memories and experiences heavily influence our emotions. But near the amygdala and hippocampus sits the prefrontal cortex, which regulates our thoughts, actions, and emotions and connects each of these to past experiences. Our brain then directs the regulation of hormones and release of chemicals into our body, affecting how we respond in specific moments.[5]

Now, at this point, you are probably asking, "Ed, why are you telling us this?" I know I'm talking about a lot of science, but this stuff is so important for us to understand, because if you aren't careful, your emotions will lead you to a cognitive bias that is not true and contradicts what the Bible says about you.

Are we not living in a world where feelings trump truth? Feelings don't make something right. The absolute truth of God's Word often stands in opposition to our feelings. If we do not address this reality, we will continue to be a culture dominated by feelings, not facts. What a dangerous place to be.

When feelings and facts stand in opposition to each other, boundaries are crossed as we begin to allow our emotions to control us, versus controlling our emotions. For example, you may experience anger that leads you to feel furious, aggressive, frustrated, or irritated. But you don't allow these feelings to dictate your response; instead, you learn to control your emotions to respond in a way that is pleasing to God.

In the medical profession, doctors and nurses often use a scale from 1 to 10 to gauge our pain. But have you ever found it difficult to express exactly what emotion you are experiencing in a given moment? It's hard to talk about emotions and feelings. So oftentimes counselors use a chart just like doctors to try to pinpoint the emotions we are experiencing.

If we don't learn to identify our feelings and understand their causes, we get tossed to and fro. We become misguided because of our cognitive biases and the filters through which we see the world. We behave very differently than the person we thought we would become.

So how do we fix this? As we have said, it cannot be to "try harder and do better." You must change the way you believe.

Why Not You? is more than just a locker room pep talk.

Why Not You? is, "God, we need a miracle to happen in our minds so You can lead us into the life You've prepared for us."

Now, one important note here: I am not undermining or diminishing what you have been through. I know your past experiences and traumas are very real. This is why we need God to help us believe differently. Despite the labels that people have placed on you that have been sticking for as long as you can remember, God is saying something different about you.

Beliefs drive our emotions, emotions drive our feelings, feelings develop moods, and if we are not careful, moods (lingering emotions) will create a state of depression or anxiety in us. People who find themselves in this place live in a reality paralyzed by fear of the unknown. If you are anything like me, you like to be in control of everything. By the way, no one is ever in control of all things (besides God). But oftentimes my anxiety comes from a place of feeling like I lack control over the outcome of a situation I am in.

When I have feelings of depression, it is often simply a lingering mood. It's hard to put into words why for three days you don't shower or brush your teeth, and have been lying in bed with no desire to get up and face the world. Or how you feel when your dad dies on your birthday, and what should be a day of celebration is suddenly the saddest day of your life.

These feelings . . . what do you do with them?

The key is to break the patterns that you currently fall back into. Most people try to escape the pain, and they chase temporary pleasure. This is how some addictions are formed. Patterns are created that become the "solution" to the pain and trauma of negative emotions and feelings. But there is a better way. For me personally, I've learned to do things like going for a run or taking a cold plunge, something that disrupts the chemical makeup of my body and is outside my normal pattern.

In the midst of negative emotions and feelings, God wants us to make choices that serve us, not harm us. But to do that, we must begin with correct thinking about what is actually happening in our lives.

What you are facing—God will bring you through it. You are going to be okay.

The world says all you have to do is change your behavior. But it's bigger than that. It starts with changing your belief. That belief is what will change your behavior and ultimately change who you are becoming.

If you don't like who you are becoming, then something has to change. You cannot keep doing what you have been doing and think that life is just going to change out of nowhere, or that you are going to change out of nowhere. You have to do something different.

> **WHAT YOU ARE FACING—GOD WILL BRING YOU THROUGH IT.**

THE PATTERN OF BEHAVIOR

Have you ever wondered how elephants at the circus are so controlled? Think about it. They are huge animals, much larger than anyone around them, and yet small humans have complete control over them.

Do you remember watching the movie *Dumbo*? I remember telling my kids it was a great movie, then remembering how sad it was when Dumbo was mistreated.

When you watch Dumbo and his mom, you wonder how the circus contains such a massive, powerful elephant.[6]

When a baby elephant is shackled to a stake and can't break free, it grows up and becomes almost larger than the tent itself, but it still believes it's unable to break the shackle. There comes a point when the circus personnel don't even drive a stake into the ground anymore. Why? Because cognitively, the elephant was trained to believe, *I can't go where I want to go.* So its whole life, the elephant feels as if it can't move.

Some of you reading this can relate. You feel like the elephant. Even though God has taken your shackles out of the ground, you are stuck feeling like you can't go anywhere, that you are still tied at the stake. The devil has kept you in shackles for far too long.

Today I want the shackles to come off. Through this journey of believing Why Not You? the shackle comes off. Jesus has broken your chains. It is time to believe the truth, not your emotions or feelings. Jesus is a chain breaker. He is setting you free to become all that God wants you to be and accomplish all that He wants you to accomplish for His kingdom.

Some of you can relate right away to the story of the elephant. Others of you might be asking, "What's the shackle?" It could be an addiction. It could be incorrect thinking. It could be something done to you or by you that labeled you and created the mindset, "I will always be this way."

But that is just not true. Jesus reminds us in 2 Corinthians 5:17, "Therefore, if anyone is in Christ, he is a new creation. The old has passed away; behold, the new has come." This is why Romans 12:2 says God renews our minds. I believe God can give you spiritual amnesia. He can start removing negative thoughts from your mind that have been keeping you down for years.

You may have been wounded so badly there is not a moment you don't think about what happened, what you did, or what you can't break free from. People say, "Just forgive and forget," but we know that is not easy to do. It is humanly impossible to forget some of what you have been through. You didn't pick it; it was done to you.

If that's you, I want you to pray this prayer:

Dear Lord, set me free today. God, if You choose not to remove the memories, I pray You would rewire the neurological pathways in my brain. When those feelings or that imagery comes—the smell, the sounds, whatever happens in that moment—please turn it around. I pray You would change it, that it wouldn't lead me down a path of destruction or into patterns that wound me. Lead me down a path of freedom and healing. In Jesus' name, amen.

This is a prayer that you can pray daily, and I want you to watch how God responds in your life. But you can't just pray this prayer and continue living in negative patterns. The patterns of behavior in your life have to change. The shackles have to come off. If you are sick of being sick, and tired of being tired, it's time to break the unhealthy patterns that lead you into those vicious cycles.

How do you do this? Let me give you a few steps to take.

1. Reject the Lies: The values you hold inform how you see yourself. Are you valuing the temporary emotions or feelings you might be experiencing, or are you valuing the truth God speaks about who you are in His eyes? Remember, all emotions and feelings are temporary, here today and gone tomorrow. God's truth never changes.

2. Break the Tendency Loops: End any coping and default mechanisms you tend to slip into by developing healthy habits. If you are held hostage by your emotions, they generate negative feelings that maintain moods that will take you down. Ask yourself, *What are my unhealthy coping mechanisms?* That high won't fix your problem. It'll leave you wanting so much more. It's escapism and you must confront it. God will give you peace this world can never give. Cling to it and let go of the unhealthy coping mechanisms.

3. Attitude Is Everything: Keep your perspective more than positive; believe that all things are possible with God. You are not stuck. Your current reality is not your final destiny. You may not be where you want to be tomorrow, but you can change yourself and your circumstances by believing the truth. God can break your shackles and put you on track to His destination for you.

Jon Bloom once said, "God designed your emotions to be gauges, not guides. They're meant to report to you, not dictate you."[7] It's time to stop letting your emotions, feelings, and moods be your boss.

I love the old quote, "Watch your thoughts; they become words. Watch your words; they become actions. Watch your actions; they become habits. Watch your habits; they become character. Watch your character, it becomes your destiny."[8]

The journey of your destiny starts with your thoughts, for right thoughts lead to the right life.

With this in mind, I'll leave you with the words of John Maxwell: "If you are willing to change your thinking, you can change your feelings. If you change your feelings, you can change your actions. And changing your actions—based on good thinking—can change your life."[9]

> **THE JOURNEY OF YOUR DESTINY STARTS WITH YOUR THOUGHTS, FOR RIGHT THOUGHTS LEAD TO THE RIGHT LIFE.**

CHAPTER 11

THE POWER IS ALREADY INSIDE YOU

AS WE CONTINUE TO UNPACK THE QUESTION, WHY NOT YOU? I want you to wrap your mind around this: Everything you need to accomplish God's perfect purpose and will for your life is already inside you. How so? Because God's power is already inside you. That power has a name, and His name is the Holy Spirit. The Spirit was Jesus' gift to us as He left the earth and returned to His Father in heaven.

John 20 tells us that Jesus came back from the dead, defeating sin, death, and hell. When He appeared to His disciples in the upper room, He walked through the door without using a handle, and they feared for their lives. But Jesus reassured them, saying, "Peace be with you" (v. 19). Once they realized it was Him, their fear turned to joy. Jesus continued: "'Peace be with you. As the Father has sent me, even so I am sending you.' And when he had said this, he breathed on them and said to them, 'Receive the Holy Spirit. If you forgive the sins of any, they are forgiven them; if you withhold forgiveness from any, it is withheld'" (vv. 21–23).

In Acts 1:3–5, we see that Jesus had set the table for His disciples ahead of time: "He presented himself alive to them after his suffering by many proofs, appearing to them during forty days and speaking about the kingdom of God. And while staying with them he ordered them not to depart from Jerusalem, but to wait for the promise of the Father, which, he said, 'you heard from me; for John baptized with water, but you will be baptized with the Holy Spirit not many days from now.'"

What promise of the Father? The one Jesus mentioned in John 16, when He said the Holy Spirit would be our helper after Jesus returned to His Father in heaven (v. 7). Now, put yourself in the disciples' shoes. These guys walked away from everything they knew to follow Jesus. Yet Jesus said He would give them this "helper" who would reveal truth; who would teach, impart gifts to, and instruct them. He even said it would be better for Him to leave. "Truly, truly, I say to you, whoever believes in me will also do the works that I do; and greater works than these will he do, because I am going to the Father" (John 14:12).

At this point, I know what you are thinking: *How can we do anything better than Jesus?* Jesus was modeling God in the flesh on earth for His disciples. By His own power, He was able to meet His own needs. But the Holy Spirit conceived, raised from the dead, baptized, and descended on Jesus; He led Jesus into the wilderness. Jesus performed miracles in His own name, yet He was trying to teach His disciples (and us) that He exhibited the supernatural and miraculous through the power of the Holy Spirit.

Don't miss this: The same power that raised Jesus from the dead lives in you today. If you are a believer, then you've given your life to Christ, and the Holy Spirit permanently dwells in you. He is your comforter, teacher, and the presence of God living directly inside you.

Yet many Christians operate with no power.

Jesus told His followers in Acts 1:8, "But you will receive power when the Holy Spirit has come upon you, and you will be my witnesses in Jerusalem and in all Judea and Samaria, and to the end of the earth."

THE POWER OF THE HOLY SPIRIT

In Acts 2 when the disciples gathered in an upper room, 120 followers of Jesus were present. Acts 2:1–4 tells it like this: "When the day of Pentecost arrived, they were all together in one place. And suddenly there came from heaven a sound like a mighty rushing wind, and it filled the entire house where they were sitting. And divided tongues as of fire appeared to them and rested on each one of them. And they were all filled with the Holy Spirit and began to speak in other tongues as the Spirit gave them utterance."

What is interesting about this manifestation of the Holy Spirit is that it fulfilled what John the Baptist spoke about Jesus. "I baptize you with water for repentance, but he who is coming after me is mightier than I. . . . He will baptize you with the Holy Spirit and fire" (Matthew 3:11).

John the Baptist was referring to the moment described in Acts 2. There were actual tongues of fire above the heads of all 120 followers of Jesus in that upper room. This was the manifestation of the Holy Spirit dwelling and residing within all 120 followers, just as John the Baptist had said it would be.

Simon Peter went from being a coward to being courageous

as he told the crowd, "Repent and be baptized every one of you in the name of Jesus Christ for the forgiveness of your sins, and you will receive the gift of the Holy Spirit" (Acts 2:38). The naysayers and critics said to Simon Peter, "You're drunk." But Simon Peter was telling them, "We got new wine." And this new wine was not the intoxication and the inebriation from over-fermented grapes but the indwelling power and presence of the Holy Spirit of God. This is why Ephesians 5:18 says, "And do not get drunk with wine, for that is debauchery, but be filled with the Spirit."

Do you remember Jesus talking with the woman at the well, the one with a pretty scandalous story? He told her, "Everyone who drinks of this water will be thirsty again, but whoever drinks of the water that I will give him will never be thirsty again. The water that I will give him will become in him a spring of water welling up to eternal life" (John 4:13–14).

If you want to achieve God's ultimate purpose for your life, the Holy Spirit will empower and unlock everything you need to live the very best version of your life. Sadly, many believers regularly choose not to access this power. They make one of two mistakes: They either grieve or quench the Holy Spirit. The Bible speaks against both.

GRIEVING THE HOLY SPIRIT

"And do not grieve the Holy Spirit of God, by whom you were sealed for the day of redemption" (Ephesians 4:30). We grieve the Holy Spirit when we have His power inside us but choose to live outside of the Word, will, and ways of God. It is when you choose to fulfill legitimate needs in illegitimate ways. When you and I grieve the Holy Spirit, it means we are not yielding to the fruit of the Spirit in our lives. Instead we are satisfying the appetites of the flesh.

We cannot walk in the power clothed in tongues of fire and experience the outpouring of the Holy Spirit while also conforming to the ways of this world. When you choose to pursue the flesh, you dampen the power and presence of the Holy Spirit in your life. When you don't walk in submission to God's perfect will and instead choose to do what you want to do, living your life on your own terms, with your own demands, desires, and cravings, you are actively grieving the Holy Spirit.

The Holy Spirit wants to radiate from you, to produce fullness of joy because of God's presence in you. But that can't happen if you decide to grieve the Spirit and chase the things of this world. That is why 1 John 2:15 says, "Do not love the world or the things in the world. If anyone loves the world, the love of the Father is not in him." It's why Matthew said, "No one can serve two masters, for either he will hate the one and love the other, or he will be devoted to the one and despise the other. You cannot serve God and money" (6:24).

But it's not just money. It's any fleshly craving. You cannot chase worldly things and have access to the unlimited power of God within you in the form of the Holy Spirit. Do you want to live out God's very best version of your life? You absolutely can. But you are going to need the limitless power that is already inside you. And to access that, you cannot grieve the Spirit.

QUENCHING THE HOLY SPIRIT

"Do not quench the Spirit" (1 Thessalonians 5:19). If you want the Holy Spirit to pour out and overflow the presence of God in and through you, you cannot "quench" the Spirit. But what does that mean?

When the Holy Spirit tells you to do something and you say something like, "They'll think I've lost my mind" or "They'll judge me and think I am a _____," you are quenching the Holy Spirit. If the Holy Spirit asks you to say something, but you live in fear and trepidation of what others might think, or you wonder if there is someone else better equipped to say it, the same is true.

When the Holy Spirit is nudging and leading you, He will give you the power to do what He is calling you to. He will give you the witness, and He will tell you what you need to say and what you need to do. He will give you everything you need in that moment. God isn't looking for a perfect person to use. He is looking for an empty vessel that will say, "Yes, Lord."

So many times we quench the Holy Spirit because we struggle to trust Him. We have salvation, our sins are forgiven, and one day we will spend eternity with God in heaven, yet we struggle to trust Him with the things He wants to do in and through us while we are here on earth.

Yet in Matthew 10, Jesus said the kingdom of heaven is at hand, and commanded His followers to heal the sick, raise the dead, cleanse the lepers, and cast out demons. But too often this is where the teaching of pastors and speakers stops. As if that supernatural and miraculous power was only for the disciples to build the early church, not for us.

We must come to grips with the fact that Jesus, who taught all of this to the disciples, is calling us with the same power He gave them. He wants to give us the courage and conviction to know that the same power that was accessible to the disciples is accessible to us, today. The power you need to fulfill your destiny is already inside you. If you have given your life to Christ, you have already entrusted Him with your forever. So why not trust Him with the here and now?

THE POWER YOU NEED TO FULFILL YOUR DESTINY IS ALREADY INSIDE YOU.

I love this quote, which is often attributed to Billy Graham: "The will of God will not take us where the grace of God cannot sustain us."[1] If God has called you to a place, a mission, a purpose, He has given you everything you need through the power of the Holy Spirit to fulfill it. The same power that was in Jesus is inside you right now. But you have to stop quenching the Spirit and believe that power is accessible to you.

WHAT IF YOU SAID YES?

Pastor Max Lucado once asked me something I will never forget. "Ed, during Christmastime, do you open every single gift that has your name on it under the Christmas tree?" Of course, I looked at him like he was crazy. I mean really, what kind of question is that? I responded, still very puzzled, "Pastor Max, of course I open up every present. Who doesn't open every present with their name on it?"

He looked at me, knowing that would be my answer, and said, "I know you do, Ed. But have you ever considered how many Christians don't open the gifts of the Holy Spirit under the tree of Calvary, and live their whole lives not knowing what could be?"

Maybe as you've read this book, you have started to think of the possibilities of what your life could be if you truly bought into the concept of Why Not Me? Not with self-confidence but God-confidence. Maybe you're starting to ask yourself questions like, *Why couldn't God use me to do all the amazing things He wants to do? What could my life look like if I said yes to His plan and purpose for me?*

Maybe you've always thought you were limited in what you could do and who you could be. You know God is going to use someone, but you assume He'll probably use someone else. But Why Not You? I hope as you have continued to read, you realize God really does want to use you to do something incredibly special. He has a unique plan and purpose for your life, one He didn't create for someone else but for you. His ultimate will for your life is that you live out that purpose and accomplish things greater than you could ever come up with in your own thoughts.

Here's the thing, though: I don't want to be a Debbie Downer, but many believers will live their entire lives and never come close to achieving all that God intended for them.

Why? Because they didn't realize that the power they needed to live out God's call was already inside them. When you give your life to Christ, there is more to it than just receiving security for your eternal home.

At the point you give your life to Jesus, you are entrusting Him with your eternity. So why not turn over your life here and now in the temporary? God doesn't just want to sell you fire insurance. He wants to use you to do something incredible.

What that is, only God can tell you. But what I can tell you is that the power you need to live out that plan is already inside you. He has given you the Holy Spirit, and that is everything you need to fulfill God's destiny for your life.

It's time to stop questioning why God doesn't choose to use somebody else. He's chosen you. It's time to stop listening to the labels that have been placed upon you, because those things are not indicative of who you are. You are God's chosen child, in whom the power of the Holy Spirit rests.

Everything you need to reach your destiny is already inside you.

CHAPTER 12

THERE IS MORE

LET ME ASK YOU A QUESTION. DO YOU WANT MORE OUT OF LIFE? Do you ever wonder to yourself, *There has to be more out there?* Or, *I want my life to be more than what I am living now?*

These are questions many people ask. Nonbelievers ask them because they don't have a personal relationship with Jesus Christ. Believers ask them when they are living outside the realm of God's will for their lives. But the uncertainty behind these questions stems from the same place. When we fail to access the power already available to us, we operate in a worldly sense, chasing worldly things that were never meant to satisfy our souls.

They leave us wondering, *Is there more to life than this?* Maybe you have found yourself asking this question, or perhaps you are asking it now. If so, I have good news for you: There is more. That "more" comes through the power of the Holy Spirit. As we discussed in the last chapter: If you are a believer, that power is already inside you.

I won't pretend that I have all the answers. I'm still studying myself, but I have tasted and seen God's power, and I know that I want more of the Holy Spirit in my life. I don't want more to be a better preacher. I don't want more to be a better pastor. I want more because I want the power of the Holy Spirit to be in my home, in my marriage, to help me raise my kids, and to manifest God's joy, peace, goodness, kindness, and gentleness in my life. I want to walk in vibrancy, vitality, and clarity. I want to keep the main thing the main thing. And I want to live my life preaching His kingdom. The life of *more* is the life of pursuing the destiny to which you were called.

There is more in store for you. But to access more, you are going to need to let the Holy Spirit, living inside you, overflow through you.

The day you gave your life to Jesus, you received the Holy Spirit and your body became a temple of the living God. Yet so many people refuse God's call. They say they want to live in freedom; instead they pursue the things of this world and end up in chains.

"Now the Lord is the Spirit, and where the Spirit of the Lord is, there is freedom" (2 Corinthians 3:17). True freedom comes from the Holy Spirit, and He is only available when we receive Christ, who said, "If anyone would come after me, let him deny himself and take up his cross and follow me. For whoever would save his life will lose it, but whoever loses his life for my sake and the gospel's will save it. For what does it profit a man to gain the whole world and forfeit his soul?" (Mark 8:34–36).

The *more* you are searching for isn't in worldly pleasures; it's not in more money, more sex, more alcohol, more real estate, more drugs, more cars, more status, or more titles. Pursuing these things is where the shackles come from. The chains you feel tied to came from chasing after these worldly pleasures to find fulfillment. They are unfulfilling; you'll always want more.

In Ephesians 3:19 Paul prayed that we would "know the love of Christ that surpasses knowledge, that you may be filled with all the fullness of God." What if you stopped looking everywhere else and realized the satisfaction and fulfillment you desperately desire are found in connection with God? How could your life change if what you really wanted wasn't "out there" but instead "in here"?

> **WHAT IF YOU STOPPED LOOKING EVERYWHERE ELSE AND REALIZED THE SATISFACTION AND FULFILLMENT YOU DESPERATELY DESIRE ARE IN CONNECTION WITH GOD?**

YOUR SPIRITUAL GIFTINGS

If you have given your life to Christ, you have the Holy Spirit living inside you. But the indwelling of the Holy Spirit is not just for salvation. It is to equip you with spiritual gifts that enable you to have spiritual growth. Every day, God is making you more like Jesus. How does that happen? Through the power of the Holy Spirit. The Spirit brings to remembrance what you have learned, giving you conviction and clarity around those things. When you read the Bible and suddenly a verse or passage pops off the page, the Holy Spirit is speaking to you. When the thought of one verse connects in your mind to another verse, the Holy Spirit is teaching you. When a name pops into your head and you have the conviction to pray for that person, the Holy Spirit is guiding you.

When you walk into spaces void of God, you bring God

with you. You bring the power of God, you bring the supernatural capabilities of God, and that all happens through the Holy Spirit pouring out through you. The Spirit enables you and moves through you. As Paul said in Philippians 2:13, "It is God who works in you, both to will and to work for his good pleasure."

How does He do this? He gives you spiritual gifts. For some, these are declarative gifts through words that we speak. For others, these are discerning gifts of wisdom, knowledge, and understanding. For still others, they are the dynamic gifts of healing, belief, and faith. No person possesses all these gifts, including you. Even so, God will give you a number of gifts unique to your calling so you can live out His perfect plan for your life. These Holy Spirit gifts give you power you otherwise would not have.

For the disciples and the 120 people in the upper room referenced in Acts 1, their power came through the clothing of tongues. The Holy Spirit, in that moment, allowed their giftings to be unleashed.

SPIRITUAL GIFTINGS

You might be asking, "Ed, do you believe in the speaking of tongues?" Yes, I do. I believe there is a prayer language. Now, every person who receives the Holy Spirit may not get that prayer language at the time they think they need it. But why do we need one? It allows us to speak to God almost in a private language. I can't explain it all—it is still new to me—but I'll tell you this: I want more of it.

Speaking in tongues is not the only gift, and no one gift is above all the others. There are many spiritual giftings, and it is our job to allow the Holy Spirit to reveal our special giftings, then seek wisdom in how God wants us to use them for His calling in our lives. Once we know the spiritual giftings that God has graciously given to us, we must continue to place our reliance upon Him, allowing the Holy Spirit to use these gifts in the way in which God intended.

This means not relying on our own power to use our spiritual gifts. It doesn't work that way. Too often, we try to live our lives in our own power, while we have been given access to the power of the Holy Spirit.

A woman once lived on the coast of Ireland at the time electricity was discovered. She was the first person, in fact, to have access to it in her area. One day, the meter reader came by her house and said, "We installed power in your home, but there is no power use registering. Why is that?"

She responded, "Oh no, it works."

Puzzled and confused, he asked her, "So, ma'am, why don't you use the power?"

She replied, "I turn on the lights at night to light my candles, then I cut the lights off."

He asked her, "So you don't use the power throughout the day?"

"No, just at night."

Now, you're probably thinking that woman was crazy. But

how often do we think and act like her? So often as believers, we only use the power in certain moments, like Sunday mornings in church. But the same power is always available to you and me:

Ex. Monday morning at work,

Tuesday night at dinner with our friends,

Wednesday at the gym when we are in a midweek slump,

Thursday when our kids want our attention, and we are depleted,

Friday night after a long, hard week, and

Saturday when we are watching football with our friends.

The power of the Holy Spirit is like electricity, except it never goes out. You have access to it now and forever, every moment, all the time. Stop using it just to light the candles. Let the Holy Spirit shine through your spiritual giftings at all times, and God will be blessed through you.

YOUR SECOND BAPTISM

The baptism of the Holy Spirit brings about many different gifts that can be fully expressed, allowing you to walk in the destiny God has called you to. You might be wondering what the *baptism of the Holy Spirit* means. Some people believe in two baptisms: one you receive at salvation and one you experience when you step into your destiny.

If you think about it, every movement of God has been marked by baptism. The Red Sea crossing was a baptism of new beginnings and freedom, breaking off the chains of slavery and hostility. Similarly, our first baptism breaks off chains through our salvation. It is the reality of sins forgiven through the power of the Holy Spirit, when He first comes to live inside us. The second baptism empowers us in the direction of our purpose and destiny, the "there is more" moment when we are empowered by the Holy Spirit to begin to live out everything God has destined for our lives. Walls fall and miracles happen.

I don't know about you, but I am tired of not walking in the power God calls me to walk in. I want to walk in a different reality. What we're learning about the power of the Holy Spirit is not a new revelation. It is just dependent on whether we will obey what the Word of God is saying.

Listen, my friend, *you are no longer a slave.* "For you did not receive the spirit of slavery to fall back into fear, but you have received the Spirit of adoption as sons, by whom we cry, 'Abba! Father!'" (Romans 8:15).

You are no longer an orphan, left to your own devices. Jesus promised us in John 14:13, "Whatever you ask in my name, this I will do, that the Father may be glorified in the Son."

You are no longer a beggar. "And these signs will accompany those who believe: in my name they will cast out demons; they will speak in new tongues; they will pick up serpents with their hands; and if they drink any deadly poison, it will not hurt them; they will lay their hands on the sick, and they will recover" (Mark 16:17–18). You are empowered by the Spirit, just as Jesus told us in this passage.

Ask yourself this question: If we are sons and daughters the King knows by name, why do we live in spiritual poverty? Why do we not live in freedom? Why do we not live in abundance and overflow?

This happens when we grieve the Holy Spirit by living in disobedience to God's Word. You can't expect miracles, signs, and wonders of God if you are not being obedient to the Word of God. When you ask God to give you a new revelation but live in disobedience, you are asking for something He won't grant you. Why would God give you a new revelation when you aren't obedient to the current one He has given you?

The moment you say, "I am not going to grieve the Holy Spirit. I am going to be obedient to what God tells me to do," the Holy Spirit now has room to do what He wants to do in and through you. And when the Holy Spirit begins to speak to you, bringing clarity and faith to believe what you are walking into, you will go from seeing things in a natural reality to a supernatural reality. You will start to know and believe God is working on your behalf behind the scenes.

Today, God wants to make you the agent of change we have been talking about. In the spaces and places where the kingdom of God does not have a presence, God wants to insert and use you in ways you could never imagine.

Henry Blackaby said, "God, you are at work around me, show me how to join you."[1] The Holy Spirit teaches us how to partner with God in this way. But if we want to join God in the work He's doing, we must stop living like spiritual orphans when we are sons and daughters of the living God.

THE OIL OF HEAVEN

In 1926, Mr. Yates, a man living in West Texas, was about to lose his ranch. He couldn't feed his livestock enough because his family was barely getting by, and the bank would soon foreclose on their land.

One day, a seismograph crew visited the ranch, wondering if his land might have a reservoir of oil on it.

The crew drilled for oil, and about a thousand feet down, they hit a reservoir full of it. Black gold. Texas tea. At that time, 450 barrels a day came gushing out of that reservoir. By 1929, it produced 204,600 barrels a day.

When I read this story for the first time, I found it so interesting. Mr. Yates was living in poverty on top of land with an unfathomable wealth of oil beneath the surface. He just needed someone to see what he couldn't.[2]

How about you? It's time to stop living in fear, timidity, anxiety, and depression, allowing your emotions to control you. When you place God at the control center of your life, the Holy Spirit will lead you into an abundant life, greater than anything you could produce on your own. Just like the experience of Mr. Yates.

The Enemy doesn't want us to have this kind of abundant life. Jesus said in John 10:10 that the Enemy comes to steal, kill, and destroy. However, he has stolen way too much from you already, mainly your belief that there is more for you to experience through the power of the Holy Spirit. The devil has given up on the fact that Jesus is the only way to heaven. When he knows he cannot steal your soul and can't take you out of the grip and grasp of Jesus, he moves on to making you think you are defeated in terms of living out your destiny while you are still on earth.

One of the best choices we can make is to properly teach and perceive the Holy Spirit's role in our lives. The Holy Spirit of God is dwelling in you, allowing you to have continuous victory after victory in your life, but the devil continues to tell you, *You can go to heaven, but I am going to cause you to live in defeat while you are still on earth.*

But if we know we win in the end, why do we live in defeat today? This happens when we aren't willing to say, "I want a fresh filling of the Holy Spirit in my life."

My friend, the oil of heaven will pour out when your vessel is empty of your pride, agendas, addictions, and so on. The Holy Spirit has no room to fill us up until we pour out what separates us from God. The things that are not enough. The things that leave us wanting more.

If you want a fresh filling, a renewal to walk equipped with and enabled by the power of the Holy Spirit, in victory and with fresh revelations, with conviction and clarity, come to God as an empty vessel. Pour out what has been filling you up. Pursue the destiny God has called you to, empowered by the Spirit. Are you ready to experience more?

CHAPTER 13

LAY IT DOWN

IN SPORTS, WE HAVE ABBREVIATED THE WORD CHAMPIONSHIP, condensing it down to just *chip*. When a professional league heads into the postseason, every team competes to "get the chip." It is a saying tied to the pursuit of winning a championship. But I want to talk about another kind of chip today, one that comes from a place of recovery. For a second, I want to get really personal with you and share my own struggle, a battle I had with depression and anxiety in December 2023.

Often we can share all our business on social media and tell everyone what we are going through, hoping someone will encourage us. But sometimes we need to be the most vulnerable right in front of somebody. That is what I want to do with you right now.

Sometimes when you begin to give testimony of what God has brought you through, it brings hope to someone else that God can bring them through a tough season as well. That is my hope for you today. I am a pastor, but that doesn't mean I don't face my own share of difficulties.

I want to share mine with you, as someone who is now walking in healing, with hopes that if you are struggling, you can find hope in the fact that God brought me through it, and He will bring you through it too. That is why it is so important to tell others what God has done in your life.

In December 2023 I experienced what was likely the darkest day of my life. I found myself sitting on the couch, with no desire to get up, in a moment of despair and discouragement.

I have battled depression and anxiety for the past several years. I am not defined by depression, nor am I defined by anxiety, but they are real struggles I face. I am now walking on a road of healing and recovery. But that December I was in a place where I felt like I didn't want to live anymore. Sitting on that couch, I was overwhelmed with emotion. There was nothing going on externally, just a whole lot going on internally.

When you are your own worst critic, you can sit in moments of insufficiency, inadequacy, and insecurity, and it all begins to pile up in front of you. For me, and maybe you have been here as well, it felt as if life would be better if I was with Jesus and not on earth anymore. I am just being completely honest with you about where I was.

You might be asking, "Ed, why are you sharing this with me?" Listen, my friend, if I can't be honest with you, how will you be honest with others? If I can't bring to you the unfortunate baggage I have carried and recognize its healing, how will you? There will come a day when someone needs to hear your story, someone looking for healing in their own life. I hope my vulnerability reminds you that you can be vulnerable with others because you never know who needs to hear your story.

As I tell you this, there is no shame on my end. This is a story of deliverance. That moment was a benchmark in my life, when I got sick of being sick and tired of being tired. Can you relate?

Are you sick of being sick? Tired of being tired? As you read this, it is no accident or coincidence that your eyes are set on the words of these pages at this very moment. You may have a divine appointment. God has you sitting here reading this book because He has a greater reality to speak about: what He wants to do in and through you.

Why Not You? is not just a mindset of "I want to be better." It's that in your life, God is doing something now. Not down the road. Not later on. God is working right now.

The question is, Will you choose to believe that's true in your life?

In the last few chapters we have been discussing the power of the Holy Spirit and the impact the Spirit has on your life. A Spirit-led life producing a Why Not You? lifestyle begins with not just belief. Over time it changes who you are becoming. But in order to change who you are becoming, you have to deal with your behaviors.

If you don't like what you are becoming, society will say to change your behavior. What I want you to understand as followers of Jesus is that if you do not like who you are becoming, then you need to change your belief. If you don't like the output, you need to change the input.

If you don't like what you are becoming or the trajectory you are on, then you need to ask yourself the question: *Do I have a big view of God or a small view of God?* When you have a big view of who God is and what He wants to do in and through you, you will begin to see yourself correctly.

We've looked at changing our beliefs. We have discussed

how to change who we are becoming. Now let's address our behaviors.

2 Timothy 3:5 says that some have "the appearance of godliness, but den[y] its power. Avoid such people."

When you read the Bible, I can't stress how important it is to read verses in the context of the chapter. It is difficult (and sometimes impossible) to truly understand what a verse is saying in isolation without understanding the verses that precede and follow it.

With that said, let's look at the verses leading up to verse 5: "But understand this, that in the last days there will come times of difficulty. For people will be lovers of self, lovers of money, proud, arrogant, abusive, disobedient to their parents, ungrateful, unholy, heartless, unappeasable, slanderous, without self-control, brutal, not loving good, treacherous, reckless, swollen with conceit, lovers of pleasure rather than lovers of God" (vv. 1–4).

Is this not an accurate description of what is happening in the world today? So often as believers we think that Timothy was addressing people outside the church. In actuality Timothy was specifically speaking to people inside it, those who have "the appearance of godliness" but deny its power. Maybe this phrase resonates with you. Maybe you have learned to speak fluent Christianese. Maybe you know how to live out the rhythms and routines of the Christian life, but you aren't walking in the power of the Holy Spirit.

There is a widely accepted but misconstrued idea that people who stand onstage at church do not face the temptations and tribulations that others face. That is nothing but a lie from the devil.

I am no different because I preach from a stage. None of us are exempt from the pain of this world. We are not defined by our struggles, but we are in a battle against them daily.

When you and I face temptations and struggles, the devil wants to isolate us and make us feel alone in them. But that just isn't true. We are all in this together.

WE ARE NOT DEFINED BY OUR STRUGGLES, BUT WE ARE IN A BATTLE AGAINST THEM DAILY.

In January I checked myself into a five-day therapy retreat in Kalamazoo, Michigan. For five days, I sat with fellow pastors and church leaders from 9:00 a.m. to 1:00 p.m., and they helped me dive into all my traumas, struggles, and depression. Let me tell you, God met me in Kalamazoo. When you go through the thick of it, God will meet you where you are.

In Kalamazoo there were these quick five- to ten-minute oil change places. But they weren't called Jiffy Lubes. They were Uncle Ed's Oil Shoppes. And their signs read "New Year, New Oil." At the time, I didn't realize they were part of a franchise. Everywhere I went, I saw these particular shops with the same sign and the same phrase, "New Year, New Oil."

When a vehicle goes into the oil change bay, the old oil is emptied, and the new oil fills the car up. Something has to be emptied so that the new oil can be put in. If you want to experience healing, you must be emptied so that the oil of heaven can flow down through you. When God met me in Kalamazoo, Michigan, He was telling me, "New Year, New Oil."

THE CHIP OF SURRENDER

Earlier we referenced the "chip" as it is used in sports. But in Celebrate Recovery—our recovery program at CBC—you gain "chips" along the way through your recovery journey. I have a lot of chips. I am a chip-carrying pastor, and I am not ashamed. But the first chip I received was the chip of surrender.

Did you grow up watching the reality show *Cops*? If you aren't familiar with it, it's a thirty-minute TV show from the '90s where cops chase criminals. That was our reality TV, quite a far cry from our current reality smorgasbord of *The Bachelor* and *The Kardashians*. *Cops* was a much simpler show. Cops chasing criminals. That was the entire show. And the same sequence occurred in every single episode.

First came the helicopter angle, spotlight on a vehicle, then sudden communication between the helicopter and the police car. The police would throw up barricades, blow the tires off a vehicle, and force the car into a ditch. You would think the bad guys would quit running, but oh no, they kept running. They would run, and run, and run. They would run for the entire thirty-minute episode. Finally, when they couldn't run anymore, they would throw their hands up in the air and wave them, showing the sign of surrender.

Maybe you have realized now that I am not just talking about a show but what happens daily in our lives. We are chased by our problems, and there comes a moment when you have to decide to say, "I surrender." There is a moment when we become tired of what we are facing and we know something has to be different, but the problem is, we keep doing the same ole thing, expecting a different outcome. You know what they call that, right? *Insanity.*

But you can lay your life down and decide to trust that God has more and better than whatever you've been placing above Him. Proverbs 3:5–6 says, "Trust in the LORD with all your heart and lean not on your own understanding; in all your ways submit to him, and he will make your paths straight" (NIV).

This is a great passage, but one many people struggle to implement. Often we don't lay things down because we don't trust God. Back in the summer of 2024, as I preached the series this book is based on, God set many people free from sins they were stuck in, and they began to throw what they were holding onto down on the altar.

At our CBC Southside campus, heroin was thrown on the altar. At the Central campus where I preach, fentanyl was thrown on the altar. Others gave up razor blades and vape pens. One weekend I held up a vape pen and said, "When we elevate something above God, we are saying that we find greater comfort in that (whatever 'that' is) than from the God who wants to do immeasurably more within us."

The devil wants to lock your arm up and keep it elevated above God, holding on tight to whatever you've been idolizing. And that is where he wants you to stay. The only problem is that there comes a point when lifting that thing up and holding it above your head becomes exhausting. The devil will encourage you to ignore the exhaustion and just keep holding it up there. But a moment comes when you end up saying, "This isn't working."

One Sunday, a lady threw a pack of cigarettes on the stage after a message in our series, and I spoke directly to her. "In about ten minutes, you are going to want those." When we lay something down, it doesn't mean the desire or craving for it goes away. So what do we do with those desires and cravings when they come? We lay them and ourselves before the Lord, as the Bible says, "Present your bodies as a living sacrifice" (Romans 12:1).

Hebrews 4:13 reminds us that nothing is unseen by God. You must lay your idols down because you must make the choice that you are going to place nothing above God and that the desires and cravings you have can be filled by God in a way that will actually satisfy your soul. Scripture makes it very clear that anything you lift above Him will never be enough.

There is a power that comes upon you when you finally make the decision to surrender and lay down your idols at the feet of Jesus. When you admit that you are struggling with something, and you lay it down, the way I laid my depression down, the way I laid my anxiety down in December 2023, there is a power that comes over you. I don't walk in shame. I walk in healing. Do you know why? Because God is a chain breaker, and I experienced His power when I finally surrendered. He broke my chains, and He can break your chains too. You are not alone in what you are going through. You can find healing in the name of Jesus when you surrender your idols at His feet.

Many years ago, as a college student, I became a lifeguard

at a summer camp pool. The rescue training was interestingly counterintuitive to what you would think a lifeguard would do. They taught us to wait until a swimmer reached the point of surrender before diving in.

We engaged in a simulation of rescuing someone who was flailing in the water. At that moment, our immediate instinct was to help because they were "drowning," but if you approach somebody fighting for survival, you have to be very careful. In the act of trying to save their own life, they may end up drowning and they can pull you down with them.

You have to wait for them to give up before you can help, but you have to be so close to them that the moment they give up, you step in. As I began to think about what it means to "lay it down," I realized that Jesus is in the water today. He is right there next to you, waiting for you to stop and receive His rescue.

LAY IT DOWN. STOP. SURRENDER.

We try to find happiness the way the world does whenever we elevate, chase, or idolize something. Sometimes we try to find happiness the way the rest of the world tries to find happiness. But God has already told us it'll never be enough.

Lay it down.

Jesus is in the water, and He's ready to save you and lead you to the life He's destined for you. So Why Not You? Well, it can be you. But not until you decide to lay down the thing you have elevated above Jesus. What do you need to lay down today?

CHAPTER 14

MIND THE GAP

MY WIFE AND I CELEBRATED OUR TWENTY-FIFTH WEDDING ANNI-versary by going to London, and it was amazing. We had an incredible time.

For those who have been to London, you know they have subways, but they don't call them subways; they call them *tubes*. You stand on a platform to wait for the train, and a gap separates the platform from the train. Signs everywhere warn passengers to "Mind the Gap," along with loudspeakers that repeat the message.

Why are they saying this? Well, if you don't pay attention, you could fall into the gap and get severely hurt because of the distance between the train and the platform.

I have been thinking a lot about the people who laid stuff down in surrender at the altar during our "Why Not You?" series in the summer of 2024, and as you think about the people who came to lay these things down in a posture of surrender, I need you to understand something: As you surrender whatever you need to lay before the Lord, when you give it to Him, a gap exists that you need to fill. Surrendering something to the Lord doesn't mean you will not face temptation or struggle anymore. In fact, the moment you lay it down, the Enemy's attack will intensify. You might even begin to question, "Well, I laid it down, but why did my struggle get worse?"

I can tell you why. The devil doesn't want you to live in a Why Not You? spirit. He wants to keep you spiritually orphaned and spiritually bankrupt. He doesn't want you to walk in the power and provision God offers you when you lay your idols at His feet.

Listen, the devil is okay with you having the appearance of godliness. He is okay with you "looking Christian." But he isn't okay with you walking in power, because when that happens, things change. Lives are suddenly impacted, not just yours but the lives of those who come into contact with you.

So when you begin to walk in power, both the power that God is working in your life and the power that you display, you show others that God can break every chain and you are living the abundant life. Yes, the devil came to steal, kill, and destroy. But Jesus came to give life and life more abundantly (John 10:10). With this in mind, know that the abundant life is not just reserved for you in heaven. God wants to give you that life here on earth. But you have to lay down the things that are keeping you from the abundant life, and then you have to fill the gaps that are left behind.

The abundant life is not just some prosperity gospel. This isn't about material stuff. I am talking about what this world can't give: peace that surpasses all understanding (Philippians 4:4 7); a God who goes with you, and who will never leave you or forsake you (Hebrews 13:5); and finding purpose in the midst of your pain. You understand that you are not alone, and God is making all things new in you.

That is a belief. And that belief will change who you become.

Unfortunately, sometimes our behavior doesn't match what we say we believe, or how God is shaping us into His vision for us. This is why minding the gap is so important. If your behaviors don't line up with your beliefs, then you have to start placing something in the gap that isn't hurting you but that's leading you to the healing God wants to give you.

Minding the gap begins with changing your mindset, and it involves understanding three key things: your triggers, tendencies, and trajectories. Let's take a look at each.

TRIGGERS

Now, you might be asking, "Ed, what are triggers?" Well, we all have them. You probably just don't refer to them as triggers. They can be external or internal experiences in life that shift our minds into a natural (cognitive) bias we carry. These biases can be based on your past, your nature, your wiring, your experiences, and your environment. These all shape how we filter what happens to us and in us. To put it plainly, something happens, and we respond based on the filters through which we view life to interpret the event and our response. We ask questions such as, *How do I respond to what just happened to me when I can't control it?* Or, *What do I do when I feel like I can't control what is happening inside me?*

Triggers lead us to turn to our bad habits, addictions, or coping mechanisms rather than turning to God. We build our cognitive biases by repeatedly responding to situations the same way, often subconsciously. If we don't seek clarity about our behavior (triggers lead to tendencies; tendencies lead to a trajectory of behavior), then we will continue to repeat the cycle. That's when change feels impossible.[1]

But the good news is, it's not! When we recognize our patterns, we can break them. That is why understanding our triggers, which might include locations, emotions, certain people, or actions/behaviors, is so important. Any of them can push us back into a bad habit or coping mechanism (tendency), creating a cycle that hurts rather than heals us.

TENDENCIES

Tendencies are coping mechanisms. They can be positive or negative, but I specifically want to speak about the negative ones we often turn to when we are triggered. You have to be really careful here because if you do not have a big view of God and you do not believe what He says about you, you might tend toward dangerous, harmful habits that lead you away from all He has for you.

This is why keeping a Why Not You? mentality is so important. It is not about building your self-confidence but your God-confidence. God has a purpose and plan for your life, not to hurt or harm you but to give you a hope and future (Jeremiah 29:11). He is making the best version of you through the power of the Holy Spirit.

But you must choose tendencies that serve His power and purposes, not tendencies that sabotage His purpose. As you lay down the thing that is keeping you from God's plans and purpose, you have to fill in the gap, and that starts with the tendencies you choose when you face triggers (locations, emotions, people, or behaviors). Romans 13:14 says, "Put on the Lord Jesus Christ, and make no provision for the flesh, to gratify its desires." God has called you to put Christ in the gap, not coping mechanisms that push you further away from Him.

To make sure I'm getting my point across, I want to give you some real-life examples of what unhealthy coping mechanisms look like:

- Hiding: You don't let anyone see the pain you are in.
- Changing Your Image: You alter yourself so others will like you.
- Denial: You pretend that nothing is wrong. "I'm good."
- Settling: "It'll always be this way. Nothing will ever change."
- Self-Sufficiency: "I got this."
- Isolation: You think no one cares about you or your struggles.
- Codependency: You find your value in helping someone else.
- Numbness: You bury everything so you don't feel anything.
- Overachieving: You think that success will fix your problems.
- Control: You try to shape every outcome.
- Staying Busy: Activity is your form of adrenaline.
- Self-Harm: You shift from emotional pain to physical pain.

- Indulgence: Food, sex, pills, porn, alcohol, workaholism, hobbies, social media, binge-watching—all forms of escapism.

Do any of these sound familiar? When we are triggered by a specific location, person, emotion, and so on, we turn to our default coping mechanisms to drown out the pain. We flail around to avoid drowning (see chapter 13). However, these coping mechanisms offer us no real solutions.

Those in the dating space know what it's like to change their image in hopes that someone will like them. We have all done this at some point or another. (Many continue to do it.) We might be truly averse to something (for example, a style or activity) but try it for ourselves in an attempt to attract or impress someone. We are willing to change so someone else will like us.

That is a tendency. Maybe you are triggered by emotions you felt when you were rejected by someone who didn't accept you as you are, so your tendency is to change for others to avoid those emotions of rejection again.

Or, when it comes to codependency, in the midst of your own trauma, pain, and struggles, you become the savior in someone else's trauma to feel better about yourself. It's not that you don't care about the person, but somehow, in helping them, you feel valuable by becoming the answer to their problem. And they become dependent on you, not God. You ignore what is going on in your own life in an effort to find healing for someone else, thus forfeiting your own healing.

What about self-harm? Have you ever wondered why people do it? A few years ago, I talked to someone who was cutting themselves. It was my first experience discussing this coping mechanism with someone using it. I said, "Explain to me why you mailed me a letter with a razor blade attached to it saying, 'I'm done with this.'" I wanted her to tell me what she was thinking in the process of cutting herself.

She told me, "In the midst of my pain, I would take a razor blade to cut myself and inflict pain. It took my attention away from my internal feelings and put it on something I could actually see."

For many, many people, the go-to coping mechanism is indulgence. It's escaping the reality of their own lives and problems only to want more, and more, and more. This includes food and overeating, sex or pornography, constantly seeking pleasure such as through a substance like weed or alcohol, scrolling on your phone to no end, playing video games, or binge-watching entertaining shows or movies.

All these forms of escapism solve nothing. They temporarily take your mind off your problems or triggers and place them on something that doesn't serve you. As Jesus reminds us, these things will never satisfy your soul (John 4:13–14).

TRAJECTORY

This cycle begins with triggers, which leads to tendencies, which then determine your trajectory in life. If you don't want unhealthy habits or coping mechanisms, what do you do? Fill in the gap by creating healthy and holy habits.

Healthy habits are the choices we must make to change direction. Learn your triggers and unhealthy tendencies, as your tendencies can lead to trajectories of addiction, isolation, constant depression, or some other negative outcome. They lead to who you are becoming. But the good news is, if you don't like your trajectory right now, you can change it.

However, you can't do this by simply changing your tendencies. You must change your beliefs by choosing to trust God, knowing that what He offers will satisfy your soul in a way no coping mechanism can.

From where you're standing, that might feel impossible. But to be blunt, feelings don't equate to reality or have the final say. Your feelings are not God. God is God. And He is the God of your feelings. Your feelings and emotions are not in control; God is. When you understand this and see God for who He is and what He sees in you, you can fill the gap with healthy habits that turn your dependence toward Him and away from what the world has to offer.

If Jesus is big enough to save you from hell, then He is certainly big enough to help you process your emotions and navigate your feelings.

Let that sink in for a moment: Our Savior, who conquered sin and death, is more than capable of walking with you through anxiety, depression, grief, anger, or confusion. He's not intimidated by your emotional struggles. In fact, He invites you to bring them to Him.

Please hear me: I praise God for doctors. I thank Him for medicine. I absolutely believe in the power of counseling and therapy. These are gifts from God, tools He uses to bring healing and wholeness. Don't shy away from them—lean into them. But at the same time, don't neglect the spiritual side of the journey.

TURNING POINT

There comes a moment, a turning point, where you've got to lay it all down before the Lord. That means getting honest with God in prayer. It means stopping the act and telling Him what you're really feeling. It's saying, "God, I don't have the strength for this. I don't even have the words. But I trust that You do. Help me."

That surrender is not weakness; it's worship. It's trusting that the God who raised Jesus from the dead can also raise your weary soul back to life. It might look like journaling your prayers, spending quiet time in Scripture, crying out during worship, or sitting in stillness and letting the Holy Spirit do what only He can do.

So yes, go to the doctor. Take the medication if needed. Schedule the counseling sessions. But don't forget to also take it to the altar. Healing is holistic, and Jesus is at the center of it all.

Listen, I praise God for doctors, medicine, and counseling. I believe in all those things. But there has to be a moment when you lay it all down before the Lord.

A day may come when you wake up and find you aren't where you want to be. You aren't who you want to be. No one wakes up and thinks, *You know what, I would love to be a drug addict today. That is the decision I am going to make today . . . to become a drug addict.* Nobody wakes up and thinks, *You know, I'd love to be divorced.* Nobody makes these decisions in a single moment. But a slow fade leads us to places we don't want to go and transforms us into people we never wanted to become.

It only takes shifting one degree off the destined path to take you somewhere you never imagined you would be. But it doesn't happen instantly; it happens over time. To put it into perspective, if you shift one degree off course and travel 12 inches, you'll miss your target by 0.2 of an inch. That might not seem like a big deal, but the farther you go, the more that one degree makes a difference. If you shift one degree off course and travel 100 yards, you'll miss your target by 5.2 feet. If you travel one mile, you'll miss your target by 92.2 feet.

Starting to make a difference, right?

If you shift one degree off course as you're traveling from San Francisco to Washington, DC, you will end up in Baltimore, 42.6 miles away. If you shift one degree off course as you're traveling around the globe from DC and back to DC, you will end up in Boston, 435 miles off. If you shift one degree off course while you're on a rocket to the moon, you'll be 4,169 miles off (nearly twice the diameter of the moon). And if you shift one degree off course while traveling to the sun, you'll miss it by over 1.6 million miles (nearly twice the diameter of the sun).[2]

All because of one degree.

Let me ask you a question: What would it look like to make a one-degree change in your life today? Jesus may be waiting for you to quit flailing your arms, lay the situation down, and mind the gap, filling in bad habits with healthy and holy habits. This means making different choices, and only two are on the shelf: pleasing God or pleasing self.

Pleasing God comes through filling your gaps with healthy and holy choices. Spiritual growth happens when you begin to make choices that prioritize what you put inside yourself. I was at a gas station not long ago, and I saw this guy who had an Escalade, and, man, was it sweet. It was blacked out. He had some 22s on there, and the rims were as shiny as could be. If you've ever driven a Cadillac, you know inside the gas lid it says Premium Grade Only. That means you can't put cheap, 87-octane inside that Cadillac. If you do, the motor will stop running efficiently.

Well, this man was putting premium fuel in his vehicle while eating a Honey Bun and drinking a Coca-Cola. He put the best of the best in the car but the worst of the worst in his body. Now, this isn't a message about nutrition, and there is nothing morally wrong with consuming Honey Buns or Coca-Cola. This is a metaphor about spiritual cleanliness. Sometimes we care more about what we put in our vehicles than what we put in our souls.

If you don't like who you are becoming, it's time to pay attention to what you're putting in your soul. It's time to notice your cycle: What triggers you? What are your tendencies?

What trajectory is that leading you on? Take some time and thoughtfully answer those questions. As you lay down some of those tendencies that are leading you to a trajectory you don't want to be on, you have to fill in the gap. And how do we fill that gap? With healthy habits and holy habits.

You can't keep doing what you are doing and expect the signs, the miracles, and the wonders to come up out of nowhere. There's got to be a change. Are you sick of being sick? Are you tired of being tired?

There are only two choices on the shelf: Are you going to please God or are you going to please you? Only one leads to the abundant life God wants to give you. It's time to mind the gap.

CHAPTER 15

STAY BATTLE-READY

ALL RIGHT, YOU'VE CHOSEN TO LIVE FOR JESUS AND GO ALL IN.
You've decided to fully surrender and "lay it down," whatever "it" is for you. You've decided you are going to mind the gap and replace negative habits with healthy and holy ones. As you make these decisions, you may find you face more opposition and fire from the Enemy than ever before.

C'mon, you didn't really think the devil was just going to hand you over and let you walk into your destiny, purpose, and calling without a fight, did you?

When you decide to fully surrender, laying down what has kept you from walking into God's purpose and calling for your life, the Enemy will begin to put you in the scope, the crossfire, the target zone, whatever you want to call it. Hell will be aimed at you.

Maybe you tried to go all in with Jesus, you tried to do the right thing, and suddenly it got really hard. You started feeling some opposition. Am I talking to you today? Maybe you decided to have that crazy faith. You wrote, Why Not You? on your mirror, or maybe you have a sticky note on your dashboard. You have chosen to believe what God believes about you. You have committed to walking in your purpose and your destiny, and you are walking into the fulfillment of what God has spoken about you.

But the moment you started walking in that direction, it

got hard. And now you are wondering, *God, I am trying to do the right thing here. Why does it have to be so difficult?*

The problem is that sometimes we equate the blessings of God with easy living. We think that the success God wants to bring into our lives should provide comfort without opposition or difficulty. But when you try to live for Him, the devil puts you right at the top of his list as enemy number one. Satan doesn't want you to experience the goodness of God that comes down from heaven and into your home, your heart, your job, or your family. However, the battle you face is not between you and the devil. This battle is in heavenly places.

Understand this: The devil is okay with you coming to church on Sunday morning. He's okay with you speaking fluent Christianese. He is fine with a "Jesus loves you" bumper sticker on your car. But when you and I understand that there is a difference between checking a box by coming to church and actually living in God's truth and presence all week long, that is when the devil starts to worry.

> THE BATTLE YOU FACE IS NOT BETWEEN YOU AND THE DEVIL. THIS BATTLE IS IN HEAVENLY PLACES.

The moment you go all in on following Jesus, you will face opposition. As you read this, you might be thinking, *Ed, how do I avoid opposition?* Are you ready for the answer?

Be a carnal Christian. See, the devil doesn't mess with people who are just going through the motions. He doesn't bother those who have one foot in the church and one foot in the world. He is okay with you "looking" godly—he just doesn't want you to access the power God offers you.

The moment you begin to walk in that power, the moment you start walking in your purpose and decide you will not be defined by your past, the moment you understand that your future has been written and it's what God has always wanted for your life, that is the moment your life goes to new levels. But with new levels come new devils. When you begin to move into an understanding of who God has made you to be, you are undoubtedly going to face opposition, challenges, and adversity.

When it comes time to face this challenge, don't look at God and ask, "Why, God? Why does this have to happen to me? Why do I have to be opposed like this?" Instead say, "Thank You that in this journey, the devil has found me to be a target because my life fully surrendered to You is a threat to hell. And because my life fully surrendered to You is a threat to hell, the demons of hell are trying to do everything they can to discourage me and defeat me."

Did you get that? Instead of asking, "Why me, God?" I want you to say, "Thank You, God!"

"Thank you? What, Ed? How could I be thankful for this?" If that's your response to this challenge, I get it. Thankfulness is not an easy mindset. But when you choose to be thankful for the opposition you're facing, you begin to see how big God is and how big His plans are for you.

In the midst of your journey, the devil will do everything he can to sabotage you and God's purpose for you. But don't make the mistake of seeing every little inconvenience as a demon. Don't be the person who believes a demon is behind everything just because you face opposition or things don't go exactly as you had planned. Sometimes things happen because we aren't disciplined enough. You can't blame a demon if you're late and having a bad day. That ain't on the devil. It's your fault you slept in.

You've got to be ready and disciplined to face the real battles. Because the moment you lock in and sync up to what God wants to do in your life, there will be difficulties. But I want to encourage you: Let your trials and tribulations testify that you are on the right track! You aren't being punished; you are headed down the road God always intended for your life.

That is why it is more important than ever that you stay battle-ready!

If you are going to stay battle-ready, there are three things you must do to win the war against your greatest enemy, the devil:

1. Know Your Covering
2. Walk in Courage
3. Speak with Confidence

Over the next two chapters, we'll take a closer look at each of these.

KNOW YOUR COVERING

Have you ever played paintball? It is a very friendly game where we shoot one another with little paintball pellets that explode, leaving marks and welts on your body as they travel over one hundred miles per hour at you. If you get hit with a paintball, you are out, and play continues until one team has no players left standing.

I was speaking at a student conference years ago, and they had an afternoon activity during free time. You guessed it, we played paintball. I will never forget that game. Now, before I go on, you must understand that there are only two types of people who play paintball. First, there are those who want to brag about the fourteen gaping flesh wounds that came from the incredible experience. If you have played, it's likely you have encountered this type of person. You know the TikTok videos people make where they say, "Tell me you _____ without telling me you _____." That's exactly what these guys are going for. They want to tell people they played paintball without ever saying it. They'll take their shirts off and maybe run into the field in flip-flops. They go full-Rambo at the paintball course.

Then there are guys like me. The guys who go to the lost and found, looking for anything they can stuff in their shirt and pants for the extra padding.

On this particular day of paintball at the conference, I walked out like the Stay-Puft Marshmallow Man. I could barely move because of all the padding and stuffing I had under my shirt. The guys asked, "Dude, what are you doing?"

I said, "You see, there is a difference between me and you: You want to get hit. I don't want to get hit. I'm not trying to walk away from here feeling the sting of a paintball on Thursday."

Before we got out on the course, the staff gave us all the typical safety instructions. If you have ever played, you know they strongly enforce keeping your goggles on the entire game. They paint the worst picture: that someone could shoot your eye out, and you would have to wear an eye patch for the rest of your life. That's truly how they warn you.

When we got on the course, I didn't want to take my paintball mask off my face, but I had a dilemma. It was fogging up. I had glasses on top of the mask, which was really complicated, and my glasses were fogging up too. I couldn't see anything.

I hid behind a tree, thinking back to the instructor's warning: "Don't take off your mask." Suddenly, I felt a hand on my shoulder. It was one of the workers at the course. He asked me, "Who are you?"

I told him, "I'm the speaker guy at this conference."

He began to raise his voice. "I don't care who you are; get off the field."

I said, "Bro, what's wrong? I was following the rules."

He said, "You've been shot forty-seven times!"

Funny story, but I didn't leave because I didn't feel any of the shots. I was so padded I couldn't feel anything.

You have an adversary who will take every angle to get at you. When you think you are good, he'll come from a different angle to try to take you out when you least expect it.

Think about this: How do you not just survive but thrive in the midst of spiritual warfare? I want you to stay battle-ready as you walk into a new purpose, a new destiny, and a fresh reality of what God has in store for you. And if you are going to do that, you have to know your covering. Like me on the paintball course, you have to be layered up. Don't be the dude walking into spiritual warfare with your shirt off. I can promise you, I would have felt the forty-seven shots if I wasn't wearing a shirt. Be the person who knows their covering.

What is your covering exactly? Well, it's your anointing and your armor. Let's take a closer look at what these two concepts mean for you on your journey of following Jesus.

Anointing

"But the anointing that you received from him abides in you, and you have no need that anyone should teach you. But as his anointing teaches you about everything, and is true, and is no lie—just as it has taught you, abide in him" (1 John 2:27).

Your gifting is different from your anointing. Gifting is the talent God has given you, your God-given ability. Talent is a God-given ability to do something that makes you different from someone else. You are gifted. Everyone is gifted. Everyone has talents. You should not have a Why Not You? mentality because of your gifts and abilities, but rather because God can do anything and everything He wants, including using you beyond your greatest imagination.

Oftentimes anointing in the church has been relegated only to people who stand on stages and hold microphones. But 1 John 2:27 says, "The anointing that you received." That doesn't mention pastors, missionaries, or worship leaders. They are included, but anointing is not exclusively for those people. *You* have been anointed.

The indwelling and baptism of the Holy Spirit are very important to your anointing. The Holy Spirit empowers your anointing with favor, to break off chains, addictions, burdens, and bondages. Your gifting makes you different from others, and people will applaud that. But when you walk in your anointing, people get set free, because it's beyond a gifting. It's living out the purpose God has placed upon your life.

When your life is empowered by the Holy Spirit, you speak value into others, helping them understand they have purpose. Your anointing is not just about you; it's about what God wants to do in other people's lives through you. Sometimes your talent and ability are just for you, but your anointing unlocks others. It sets people free. When you speak, they receive something. When you do what you do and live how you live, fully immersed, saturated, and marinated in the Holy Spirit of God, you are walking in and living out your anointing in a way that affects the lives of those around you.

When you put on display your giftings and talent, people may say, "Man, he is so good at what he does." Or "She is so gifted." They recognize it. But often the focus is on you.

Your anointing is not meant for you to walk around flexing on everybody. When you walk in the anointing of God in your life, it is not about your strength. It's God using His strength to make a difference in somebody's life. The anointing of God in your life is not so you can walk around and go, "Look at me." Instead it becomes, "Look at Him and what He has done in my life, that I can walk in power despite the strongholds, addictions, traumas, and everything that held me in bondage just a short time ago."

When you walk in your anointing, you walk in the supernatural ways of God, and He has the space to do in and through you what you could not do with your talent alone.

Armor

"Put on the whole armor of God, that you may be able to stand against the schemes of the devil" (Ephesians 6:11). When you look at this verse, you see that we need not just our anointing but the armor of God to be able to stand against the schemes of the devil. You might ask, "Ed, what are the schemes of the devil?" These are the strategies in which he will use your own tendencies (as we discussed in chapter 14) against you.

The devil knows your appetites and cravings. He knows what will trigger you and how to draw out the tendencies within you. He knows what you will likely fall back into if you do not stay battle-ready.

Often, what we feel externally or experience internally is based on our perception. When you face certain situations, your mind creates the frame or lens through which you view life. How you frame it can become your future in it.

Perhaps you have been living in spiritual defeat versus victory because the devil knows your triggers. He knows right when to put that one temptation in front of you. And because of your cognitive bias, you fall back into the same sin over and over again.

It's the same ploy he has been using since Genesis. From

the very first sin in the garden, the devil was essentially saying, "Keep your eye on the one thing you can't have and miss out on all the good God wants you to have."

Does that not seem like the exact situation he puts us in time and time again? The devil loves to use your triggers against you. If your mindset is "If it feels good, it must be good," you have no chance. Your feelings will lead you astray. Your biases will lead you to want to fulfill the legitimate needs in your life in illegitimate ways—ways the Bible says is wrong. It might feel good in the moment. That's what sin does. Sin feels good for a moment, but it always leads to pain. There comes a time when you realize that that sin is not enough. So you search for a new pleasure or a new high. Your tendencies then end up producing the same empty outcome. After all, when you keep doing what you are doing, you are going to keep getting what you are getting.

I have a profound statement for you. Are you ready for this?

If nothing changes, *nothing changes.*

You have to change how you see things so you can change how you perceive what is going on in your life. God wants you to flip the frame.

When you flip the frame, you make the decision to trust God. The reason you can trust God is because He is good. That doesn't mean you always feel good, but you can be assured God is always working for your good. Practically speaking, how do you do this? How do you change your perspective and see things the way God wants you to see them and not through the triggers the devil is placing in front of you?

You have to put on the whole armor of God.

Let's look at what the armor of God includes.

THE HELMET OF SALVATION: Where is the battle? It's in your mind. Therefore, to protect your mind, you must wear a helmet. What you believe about yourself all begins with the mind. Having a sound mind begins with the assurance of what God says about you and claiming that on a daily basis.

BREASTPLATE OF RIGHTEOUSNESS: God, throughout Scripture, reminds us that our sins are forgiven. They have been thrown into the depths of the ocean, removed as far as the east is from the west. 1 John 1:9 tells us, "If we confess our sins, he is faithful and just to forgive us our sins and to cleanse us from all unrighteousness." You are righteous. You are holy. You are chosen in Jesus' name. Claim these promises today and walk in righteousness.

BELT OF TRUTH: Truth holds everything together. We live in a world that struggles with truth. We like to think, *What's true for you might not be true for me,* so we "agree to disagree." It's really cute to believe that way, because it's nonconfrontational. But it gets confrontational when somebody gets hurt, and you need justice.

As my good friend Chris White said, "Truth, void of any form of emotion, sometimes becomes just legalism and religion. But emotion with no truth will lead to chaos."[1] We are living in a day where we are led by our feelings, and if I could give a word that gives an accurate description of where we are in this world right now, it would be *chaos.* God's purpose for you is established in truth, which is why if we're going to put on the full armor of God, we cannot forget the belt of truth.

SHIELD OF FAITH: Faith yields effectiveness. In Ephesians 6 Paul not only talked about the schemes and strategies of the devil, but he also mentioned the arrows the Enemy shoots at you. They have been dipped and pitched, then lit on fire, so even if they hit a shield, they deflect and cause damage to something (or someone) else. If the devil can't hit you, he hopes to hit someone close to you.

But in biblical times, leather covered a shield. When an arrow struck it, it would stick, not deflect. In the same way, your faith is the shield that protects you against the lies of the devil and his attempts to hurt not only you but those closest to you.

SWORD OF THE SPIRIT: The sword is the Word of God. To combat the devil, you must implement what Jesus tells you. He taught us, when He faced temptation in the wilderness, that His Word has power. It will defend you and attack the devil.

SHOES OF THE GOSPEL: Soldiers in biblical times wore cleats. Why? Because sometimes the ground became slippery. When it comes to spiritual battles, the ground can also get slippery, and the Enemy will try to push you off the ground you're standing on. That is why the Lord says to stand firm with the shoes of the gospel. This is how you "know your covering."

Do you want to walk into the purpose God has for your life? It won't come without opposition. Stay battle-ready!

CHAPTER 16

WALK IN COURAGE AND SPEAK WITH CONFIDENCE

AS HARD AS IT IS TO IMAGINE, BACK IN THE DAY, I WAS A BALLER. If you know me, have seen me, or have listened to me speak, you might question whether I was ever actually an athlete. I'm here to tell you that despite how I look now, there was a time when I was. And I loved to play basketball.

Some of my greatest life memories were in the gym with my teammates and coaches. My high school coach used to say this for motivation: "Newton?"

"Yes, sir?"

"Remember, when you are not practicing, somewhere someone *is* practicing. And when you meet him, he will win."

So I woke up every day, driven to be the best. I put in the work. I had that "no days off" mentality.

Maybe you have heard that quote even if you aren't a basketball player. It doesn't just apply to basketball or even sports in general. It also applies to life.

There are no vacation days in spiritual warfare.

The demons and the devil the Bible speaks of don't give you the weekend off. The devil won't take it easy on you because you have had a hard month. He wants to maximize every moment in your life and leverage it against you. This is why the Bible teaches us the

THERE ARE NO VACATION DAYS IN SPIRITUAL WARFARE.

principle of staying battle-ready: "Be sober-minded; be watchful. Your adversary the devil prowls around like a roaring lion, seeking someone to devour" (1 Peter 5:8).

Being sober-minded means staying alert and ready because you never know when the devil will use your triggers and tendencies to keep you on a destructive trajectory, one you may have traveled for far too long.

Do you want a new trajectory? Do you want the trajectory God is calling you to as you step into His purpose and plan for your life?

WALK IN COURAGE

To quote the great John Wayne, "Courage is being scared to death, but saddling up anyway."[1] Courage is not the absence of fear. It is choosing, no matter what you see, to frame your circumstances correctly. What you face may be bigger than you, but it's not bigger than God.

God is bigger than our greatest fears, bigger than any situation we will ever experience. Bigger than the challenges, trials, and opposition the devil puts in front of us. Joshua 1:9 tells us, "Have I not commanded you? Be strong and courageous. Do not be frightened, and do not be dismayed, for the LORD your God is with you wherever you go."

How do you walk in this courage God is talking about? There has to be a shift. You have patterns of allowing triggers to lead to tendencies that have you on a trajectory you don't like. If you are going to change the output, it starts with changing the input. And that takes courage.

If you are going to walk in the courage that Jesus has called you to, there are three things you have to understand:

1. Remember the battle doesn't belong to you; it belongs to the Lord.
2. Adopt a "buffalo mentality."
3. Reject shame and truly believe it is not who you are.

The Battle Belongs to the Lord

If you frame correctly the God you serve, you realize that He is bigger than every giant you will face. I want to speak something over you that should give you a little peace right now: The God you serve is bigger than anything you could ever face. He's bigger than your situation, and He is bigger than your battle.

Now, it's great to know that God is bigger, but how do we use that information? What does that mean for us in this battle against the opposition? My friend, what it means is that the battle you are facing belongs to the Lord. The battle is not yours.

The financial battle, the medical battle, the relational battle, whatever you have going on in your world, that is your battle. And in the midst of that battle, the Word of God speaks over your life that God is not only bigger than the battle you face, but *the battle is not yours.* 2 Chronicles 20:15 says, "For the battle is not yours but God's."

You can't fix it. You can't control it. You can't strategize enough to win it. The reality is, you can't do anything about it. You have to do what you can do (the part God has called you to do, being obedient to Him), and then when you realize you can't do anymore, you have to turn it over to Him.

The battle is His.

Buffalo Mentality

Okay, so when you read this subhead, I'm guessing it sparked your interest. You're probably thinking, *What is a buffalo mentality?*

Two similar animals exist together in the pasturelands of Colorado: buffalos and cows. Yet one interesting difference between them shows up when a storm comes. Cows run from the storm; buffalos run to it.

Maintaining a buffalo mentality means confronting trials and opposition when they come toward you. I run to the storm because if I run to it, I can run through it. If you run from it, you will always be in it. It will chase you.

Instead of running from the storm, when you run to it and become the storm confronter, you face it head-on. Some of us continue to experience the same storm over and over, with the same results for decades, because of a cow mentality. We run from the storm.

You expect a different outcome but won't do anything different. Remember what we said in the previous chapter? If nothing changes . . . nothing changes. You have to flip the frame, knowing that God is bigger than any battle you are facing. God is the undefeated, unblemished heavyweight champion of the world. And He is fighting on your behalf. When you call on the name of Jesus, He causes the devil to flee and tremble. Call on that name. Have a buffalo mentality. No situation is greater than the God you serve. Run *to* the storm so you can run *through* it.

Shame Is Not Who You Are

People will sometimes frame you. We know that by now. They will do this to you by remembering and keeping you in the worst moments of your life, and they'll tell everyone about it. The one moment where you know you messed up. The one moment where you wish you could get a do-over. The one where you ask yourself, *What was I thinking?* They might even have others framing you according to that same moment.

We adopt shame when our mistake becomes our identity. If you resonate with this, I want to encourage you: Shame has no place in the life of a child of God. Yes, you blew it. But the Bible says in Proverbs 24:16, "For the righteous falls seven times and rises again." Even though people will frame you in that moment, you serve a God that breaks that frame and says, *No, no, no, there are a whole lot more snapshots of what I am moving you toward.*

People will try to leave you right there where they framed you. They will bring it up every time they are around you. It doesn't matter how many times you say you're sorry, they will continue to bring it up because that is how they keep power over you.

You must get to a place in your life where you have done all that you can to make it right, and then give it to God. You cannot continue to see yourself the way they try to frame you. You might need to address the issue directly and say, "I am sorry for what I did. I made a mistake. But I can't keep seeing myself as you do. You are not the filter I see myself through. I wish I could get a do-over. I wish I wouldn't have done it. But my God didn't leave me in that mistake. He is still working on me and changing me, and I will not allow your view to define who I am."

For some people, apologies will never be enough. They will slander you, gossip about you, and continue to leave you in that same frame. Many of you are still living in their distorted frame. If that's you today, God wants to break the chain of shame in your life. If you are going to step into the belief of Why Not You?, truly accepting the truth that God wants to use you to live out the most incredible plans and purpose for your life, you have to leave the shame at the door. Let it go, and let God define who you are.

SPEAK WITH CONFIDENCE

As you seek to stay battle-ready against the opposition, you must not only *know your covering* and *walk in courage*, but you also must *speak with confidence*. Psalm 141:3 says, "Set a guard, O LORD, over my mouth; keep watch over the door of my lips!"

LET IT GO, AND LET GOD DEFINE WHO YOU ARE.

If you really think about it, nobody speaks more to you than *you*. Have you ever thought about that? There is nobody you listen to more than you. With that in mind, let me ask you a question: How do you speak to yourself?

We have to get to a place where we understand the power of words and the effect they have on our lives. This goes beyond the idea of positive vibes. It isn't a New Age concept. If I were in a public setting and yelled, "Fire!" it would cause panic. People would scramble for the nearest exit with serious urgency. That is because words have power. That is why the psalmist warned us about how we use our mouths. There is life and death in the power of the tongue.

Often we build up everyone else while constantly tearing ourselves down. We don't speak the same way to ourselves as we do to others. Yet our words reveal our faith. "Out of the abundance of the heart his mouth speaks" (Luke 6:45). When we say things such as "I'm stupid. I'm ugly. I'm a failure. I'm good at nothing. I'm not worthy of good things. I'll never be loved. I'll never be successful," we affect ourselves and our lives. We start to truly believe these things. Have you ever said anything like this?

When I spoke to our church about how to stay battle-ready, I wrote down exactly what I just listed: "I am stupid. I am ugly. I am a failure. I am good at nothing. I am not worthy of good things. I am never going to be loved. I am never going to be successful." But the moment I wrote those phrases down, it was like divine intervention came over my heart. I noticed that everything read "I am . . . I am . . . I am . . ." All of it was lowercase.

Then I flipped the frame. I believed what God says about me. I wish I could walk up to you right now and show you this personally.

I started writing what the Word of God says about me. "I *am* accepted. I *am* never alone. I *am* holy. I *am* forever loved. I *am* fearfully and wonderfully made. I *am* forgiven. I *am* free. I *am* chosen. I *am* His workmanship. I *am* strong. I *am* bold. I *am* a new creation."

When I wrote those phrases, I wrote "I *am*." Not because I am somebody worthy of all these things, but because *He* is the great I AM.

He says all of this about you too. We have said time and time again that the idea of Why Not You? is not rooted in self-confidence but God-confidence, when we choose not to believe the labels and framing others have placed upon us but the truth God has spoken over us.

If you are going to truly live in a Why Not You? state of mind, believing God wants to use you in powerful ways to do unimaginable things, you are going to have to *walk in courage* and *speak with confidence.*

Courage is not simply mustered out of thin air. Your confidence is not in empty words. God wants to use *you* and remind you that, through Him, you are all that He says you are: "I *am* accepted. I *am* never alone. I *am* holy. I *am* forever loved. I *am* fearfully and wonderfully made. I *am* forgiven. I *am* free. I *am* chosen. I *am* His workmanship. I *am* strong. I *am* bold. I *am* a new creation."

Accept the truths God has placed over you. Reject the framing and negative beliefs you have allowed to reign over you for far too long. Walk today in courage, speaking with confidence, knowing the Enemy and the opposition he places in front of you are not big enough to conquer the God you serve. The battle is His, and where He has called you, He will lead you! Stay battle-ready.

CONCLUSION

WHAT DO I DO NOW?

AS WE TAKE THE IDEAS AND TRUTHS WE HAVE LOOKED AT throughout this book and try to fully grasp this idea of Why Not You?, I want you to understand something: Why Not You? is a statement of belief. It is choosing to believe what God believes about you. God wants you to believe what He believes and receive what He wants to give you. As we have said so many times throughout the book, Why Not You? is not about self-confidence. This is not a self-help or motivational book. Why Not You? is about having God-confidence, walking in faith, promise, and truth. God is for us. He's faithful to us. And He's fighting our battles.

We must stop living with a low view of ourselves and a low view of God. You serve a big God who is bigger than every giant you will ever face. God is good. Why Not You? is about you walking into that destiny and believing what God believes about you.

Have you ever heard the term *third string*? *Third string* is used in sports to describe the third person in order of who plays at a particular position. It is most commonly used in football, though it can be used in other sports. You have the starters, then you have the second string, which is the first substitute for the starters, and then there is the third string.

To put it bluntly, if you're third string, that means you

don't play much. I know exactly what that feels like. When I played college basketball—until my senior year, when I got the opportunity of all opportunities—I was third string. I didn't play unless we were winning by a lot, losing by a lot, or a lot of people in front of me were hurt.

There is an urban legend of sorts about a football player named "Third String."[1] Third String had played four years of college football but never got the chance to play. On the team's depth chart, he was always, you guessed it, third string.

But at the end of his senior year, following the regular season, his team had earned the right to go to a bowl game. This was a big deal, as the team would travel somewhere across the country to play.

As the time came for the team to step on the bus, just five days out from their bowl game on Saturday, the coach and his assistant pulled aside Third String to give him some shocking news. "Young man, we have to talk to you."

Third String had a feeling this was bad news. With a pit in his stomach, he looked at his coach and responded, "Yes, sir?"

"Son, we are so sorry to tell you this, but we've received word from your mom that your dad has passed away. Now, I don't want you to worry about this game. You need to go home, be with your mom and sisters, and honor your dad," the coach told him.

Third String said, "Yes, sir."

Third String went home and loved on his mom and sisters, doing everything he could to comfort them. They had an incredible memorial service, as good as you could have asked for, given the circumstances. It definitely honored his dad.

But then, as Saturday approached, Third String felt in his spirit that he needed to get to that stadium. So he found a way to get there. Car, plane, cab—he did everything he could to get to that locker room and prepare for the bowl game, the final game of his playing career.

When he arrived at the locker room, he was able to get all the equipment he needed. He put on a uniform, but the jersey didn't have his last name on it. It was an extra, there just in case. He had everything he needed and got laced up and ready to go.

He walked out the tunnel and onto the field; his teammates couldn't believe their eyes. They knew Third String's father had passed; it was the reason he was absent from practice all week leading up to the game.

Third String walked up the sideline and spoke to nobody. With resolve in his eyes and focus as never before, he approached the coach, took out his mouthpiece, and insisted, "Coach, I have to play today."

Completely alarmed, his coach said, "Son, what are you doing here?"

Third String said it again. "Coach, I've got to play today."

The coach could see how locked in and serious he was. Realizing something was brewing in this young man's heart, he leaned over to the special teams coach and told him to put Third String in on the kickoff team.

If you know anything about football, you're familiar with the three core units of offense, defense, and special teams. The special teams unit is often, though not always, the least consequential. This was a way for the coach to get Third String in the game in a very low-stakes type of way. The special teams coach told Third String, "Just run down the field and hit somebody." Wouldn't you like those instructions? Just run and hit somebody?

After being put on the kickoff team, Third String waited for his moment. As the ball was kicked off, he sprinted as fast as he could. Beating everyone down the field, Third String was the first person to get to the return man, hitting him so hard that he fumbled the ball. Guess who recovered the fumble? Third String.

As he came off the field, he handed the ball to the referee and looked his coach dead in the eyes, saying, "I told you I had to play today."

Suddenly the coach wanted to give Third String more opportunities. *Where has this been?* the coach thought. He put Third String in the game in all three units: offense, defense, and special teams.

At the end of the game, the game's sponsor handed out an award for the MVP (Most Valuable Player). It was Third String. Everyone was stunned. No one had even heard of this guy. The reporters were trying to find him for an interview, but he was nowhere to be found.

Finally, they spotted him in the end zone with his helmet still on, chin strap fastened, mouthpiece in, tears flowing down his face. The coach broke through the crowd and grabbed Third String by his face mask, lifting him up to eye level.

The coach looked at him and said, "Son, for four years you've been on this team, and I've never seen you play like that."

Third String took out his mouthpiece to speak, and he said, "Coach, on Monday you told me that my daddy died. But you didn't know my dad; he was blind. All my life, my dad has been at every game. Pop Warner, middle school, high school, and even college. He sat in the stands and cheered for me, and he never got the chance to watch me play. But my dad was a Christian, and the moment he gave his life to Jesus, he was destined for heaven. Coach, I had to play today because this was the first time my dad could ever see me play. And all I could hear in my ears was my daddy saying, 'Go, son, go!'"

"Go, son, go!"

"Go, son, go!"

"Go, son, go!"

"Go, son, go!"

I wrote this book so you could hear your heavenly Father say, "Go, son, go!" "Go, daughter, go!"

Run! Run with everything you've got.

Hebrews 12:1–2 says, "Therefore, since we are surrounded by so great a cloud of witnesses, let us also lay aside every weight, and sin which clings so closely, and let us run with endurance the race that is set before us, looking to Jesus, the founder and perfecter of our faith, who for the joy that was set before him endured the cross, despising the shame, and is seated at the right hand of the throne of God."

God has called you to a greater purpose for your life. We have said from the beginning that He is going to use somebody to do something great. *Why Not You?* Why can't you be the one God uses to live out the destiny He designed for you and change not only your own life but the lives of those who come in contact with you?

Why Not You? is not about you. It's about a God who wants to use you for a greater purpose. That purpose is not just to help you but to help you help others and bring glory to God's name. Today God is telling you, *Go, son, go! Go, daughter, go!* It's time for you to believe what God believes about you and walk in this Why Not You? mentality—that God is going to do incredible things in and through you.

So, again, Why Not You? You are anointed. You are chosen. You are enough. Believe what God believes about you. Don't wait for perfection—walk in faith. The power is already within you. Lay down your doubts, step into your calling, and watch God do something extraordinary through your life.

ACKNOWLEDGMENTS

FIRST AND FOREMOST, TO MY BEST FRIEND, MY LOVE, AND MY greatest encourager, Stephanie. From the very beginning you have believed in me, prayed for me, and stood by my side through every season. Your unwavering faith and steadfast love have been my anchor, and I am beyond grateful to walk this journey with you.

To our four incredible children, you are my greatest blessings. Each of you is a gift from God, and my deepest desire is that you walk boldly in the fullness of who He has called you to be. May you always know that His plans for you are greater than anything you could imagine and that you were created for such a time as this.

To my parents, who are now in heaven, you raised me with love, resilience, and a deep commitment to Jesus. Though you navigated the world in silence, your lives spoke volumes through your faith, sacrifice, and devotion. Thank you for pointing me to Christ and showing me that strength is found in surrender. Your legacy lives on in me, and I am forever grateful.

ACKNOWLEDGMENTS

A special thank you to Tiffany Brown, Tori Jones, Kristen Cave, and Brett Camp, who helped bring this book to life. Your dedication, insight, and hard work have been invaluable in shaping these words into a message that I pray will inspire and encourage many.

To everyone who has been part of this journey: family, friends, and the Community Bible Church family. Thank you for your love, prayers, and encouragement. This book is not just my story but a testimony to God's faithfulness in all our lives.

To the One who makes the impossible possible, Jesus Christ, may all the glory be Yours.

NOTES

CHAPTER 1

1. "Walk Like an Egyptian," track 4 on the Bangles, *Different Light*, Columbia Records, 1986.
2. *Slumdog Millionaire*, directed by Danny Boyle (Fox Searchlight Pictures, 2008).

CHAPTER 2

1. Craig Groeschel, *Winning the War in Your Mind: Change Your Thinking, Change Your Life* (Zondervan, 2021), 86.

CHAPTER 3

1. Mythili Ramesh, "Never Settle: The Inspiring Story of an Old Watch and Self-Worth," Medium, September 24, 2020, https://mythiliramesh.medium.com/never-settle-the-inspiring-story-of-an-old-watch-and-self-worth-102a43861922.

CHAPTER 4

1. *Madam Secretary*, season 4, episode 22, "Night Watch," written by Barbara Hall and David Grae, directed by Rob J. Greenlea, aired on May 20, 2018, CBS.
2. Max Lucado, *You Are Special* (Crossway Books, 1997), 28.

CHAPTER 5

1. Jim Holt, "Time Bandits," *New Yorker*, February 20, 2005, www.newyorker.com/magazine/2005/02/28/time-bandits-2.

2. Tom Hanks, interview by Terry Gross, "Tom Hanks Says Self-Doubt Is 'A High-Wire Act That We All Walk,'" *Fresh Air*, aired on NPR, August 29, 2016, https://www.npr.org/2016/08/29/491800907/tom-hanks-says-self-doubt-is-a-high-wire-act-that-we-all-walk.

3. Barbara Corcoran (@barbaracorcoran), "Who doesn't suffer from imposter syndrome? Even when I sold my business for $66 Million, I felt like an absolute fraud!" Instagram, February 25, 2020, https://www.instagram.com/p/B9AzPs3nhmA/.

4. Daniel Schorn, "Transcript: Tom Brady, Part 3," 60 Minutes, CBS News, November 4, 2005, https://www.cbsnews.com/news/transcript-tom-brady-part-3/.

5. C. S. Lewis, *Mere Christianity*, rev. ed. (HarperSanFrancisco, 2001), 136–137.

CHAPTER 6

1. Ian Simkins, "A Sermon on Imposter Syndrome and Identity," posted July 10, 2023, by The Bridge Church, YouTube, 34 min., 53 sec., https://www.youtube.com/watch?v=AZ7jJbdA3ys.

2. Peter Scazzero, *Emotionally Healthy Spirituality: Unleash A Revolution in Your Life in Christ* (Zondervan, 2006), 40.

3. Henry Ford, *My Life and Work*, collaboration with Samuel Crowther (Doubleday, Page & Company, 1923), introduction, 19.

CHAPTER 7

1. "Boulevard of Broken Dreams," track 4 on Green Day, *American Idiot*, Reprise Records, 2004.

2. "Joseph's Colorful Coat," Ligonier Ministries, July 2, 2007, https://learn.ligonier.org/devotionals/josephs-colorful-coat.

3. T. D. Jakes, "Beware of 3 Types of Friends," LIVE FOR JESUS,

YouTube, April 9, 2020, 7 min., 54 sec., https://www.youtube
.com/watch?v=2M3vzM8YT4o.

4. Arthur Toole, "3 Types of People (From T. D. Jakes),"
arthurtoole.com, December 7, 2016. https://www.arthurtoole
.com/3-types-of-people-from-t-d-jakes/.

CHAPTER 9

1. Caroline Leaf, *Switch On Your Brain: The Key to Peak Happiness,
Thinking, and Health* (Baker Books, 2013), 13–35.

2. Leaf, *Switch On Your Brain*, 13–35.

3. Caroline Leaf, *The Perfect You: A Blueprint for Identity* (Baker
Books, 2019).

4. Craig Groeschel, *Winning the War in Your Mind: Change Your
Thinking, Change Your Life* (Zondervan, 2021), 115–126.

CHAPTER 10

1. Donna Kersey, "The Storms in Life," God's Other Ways, last
modified March 25, 2020, https://www.godsotherways.com
/stories/2020/3/25/do-the-next-thing-4baw5-racbn.

2. Joseph Prince, *Spiritual Warfare* (Joseph Prince Teaching
Resources, 2005), 110.

3. Jonas Polfuß, "Are There 34,000 Human Emotions?
Deconstructing Patterns of Scientific Misinformation,"
Accountability in Research, August 2024, https://doi.org/10.1080
/08989621.2024.2393813.

4. Varsha N. et al., "Chemistry of Emotions—A Review,"
*International Journal for Modern Trends in Science and
Technology* 6, no. 10 (2020): 26–30, https://doi.org/10.46501
/IJMTST061005.

5. Joseph LeDoux, *The Emotional Brain: The Mysterious
Underpinnings of Emotional Life* (Simon & Schuster, 1998),
138–178.

6. *Dumbo*, directed by Ben Sharpsteen, et al., (Walt Disney
Productions, 1941).

7. Jon Bloom, "Your Emotions Are a Gauge, Not a Guide" Desiring God, August 3, 2012, https://www.desiringgod.org/articles /your-emotions-are-a-gauge-not-a-guide.

8. Frank Outlaw, as quoted in *The Best of Bits and Pieces,* ed. Arthyr F. Lenehan (Economics Press, 1994).

9. John Maxwell, *Thinking for a Change: 11 Ways Highly Successful People Approach Life and Work* (Center Street, 2005), 5.

CHAPTER 11

1. Billy Graham, Goodreads, accessed May 10, 2025. https://www .goodreads.com/quotes/199683-the-will-of-god-will-not-take -us-where-the.

CHAPTER 12

1. Henry Blackaby et. al., *Experiencing God: Knowing and Doing the Will of God,* (B&H Books, 2021) 65.

2. Julia Cable Smith, "The History and Impact of the Yates Oilfield in Pecos County," Texas State Historical Association, updated July 16, 2016, https://www.tshaonline.org/handbook/entries /yates-oilfield.

CHAPTER 14

1. Brad Wolfe, "Understanding Harmful Habits: The Psychology Behind Our Actions," *Reimagine* (blog), November 30, 2023, https://letsreimagine.org/blog/understanding-harmful-habits -the-psychology-behind-our-actions?

2. Antone Roundy, "A Mere One-Degree Difference," *The Art of Ethical Persuasion, White Hat Crew* (blog), n.d., https:// whitehatcrew.com/blog/a-mere-one-degree-difference/.

CHAPTER 15

1. Chris White, conversation with the author, Shocco Springs, Alabama, 2008.

CHAPTER 16

1. *John Wayne's Book of American Grit: Stories of Courage and Perseverance Throughout Our Nation's History*, ed. Tim Baker et al., Media Lab Books, 2020.

CONCLUSION

1. "The Father's Eyes," Bible.org, July 20, 2009, https://bible.org /illustration/fathers-eyes.

ABOUT THE AUTHOR

DR. ED NEWTON SERVES AS THE LEAD PASTOR OF COMMUNITY Bible Church (CBC) in San Antonio, Texas. Since assuming this role in January 2016, he has been dedicated to fostering a multigenerational and multicultural community committed to being the good news of Jesus to every person in every place.

Raised in Orlando, Florida, as the only child of two deaf parents, Ed's early life was marked by unique challenges and profound experiences. Acting as his parents' primary communicator, he developed a deep empathy and understanding for those often marginalized by society. These formative years instilled in him a passion for inclusivity and a heart for the overlooked.

Ed's journey to ministry was shaped by personal adversity and a transformative encounter with faith during his high school years. Despite academic setbacks, including a low score on the SATs, he pursued higher education, earning a bachelor of science in church ministries from Clearwater Christian College. He further obtained a master's degree in religious education from Mid-America Baptist Theological Seminary, and a master of divinity and a doctorate of ministry in pulpit communication from Trinity Theological Seminary.

Before his tenure at CBC, Ed served as an evangelist, speaking all over the country. His dynamic communication style, characterized by passion and authenticity, resonates across diverse audiences. Beyond preaching, Ed is an accomplished author. His latest book, *Why Not You? Believing What God Believes About You*, continues his mission to inspire individuals to embrace their God-given potential.

Ed resides in San Antonio with his wife, Stephanie, and their four children.

For more information on Ed's ministry, speaking engagements, or to access his latest sermons and resources, visit ednewton.com.